CW01584418

VILLAGE S
a
BEYOND

From Pupil to Teacher 1906–1923

HUBERT CHAPMAN

From East Claydon School in Buckinghamshire to Culham College in Oxfordshire

The Book Castle

BB

First published July 1996
By Brundall Books

Distributed by
The Book Castle
12 Church Street
Dunstable
Bedfordshire LU5 4RU

© Hubert Chapman 1996

ISBN 0 9518217 1 7

Designed by Trevor Wood, Houghton Regis, Beds.
Computer Typeset by Keyword, Aldbury, Hertfordshire
Printed and Bound by Antony Rowe Ltd., Chippenham, Wilts.

All rights reserved.

CONTENTS

Front cover: Lark Rising – a watercolour done at East Claydon School by the author for the Infants' Calendar for June 1916

Dedicated to the memory of:

JOHN ALFRED WHITE

JOHN THOMAS READ

and

ARTHUR CHARLES WALTER

Village Schoolmasters

FOREWORD

Very many thanks are due to my daughter Gillian Spencer and to Lizzie Calder and Patricia Bell who encouraged me to write, in my latter years, an account of my schooldays and how I became a teacher in the early years of this century.

I am grateful to friends in Botolph, East, Middle and Steeple Claydon and particularly to the headteacher of East Claydon First School, Mrs Jill Hubble, for help with illustrations. I am grateful to the Archivist of Culham Educational Foundation, Mr Brian Seyer, for photographs of and information about Culham in my day.

My daughter Gillian edited and prepared this book for publication. Without her it would not have seen the light of day.

The dedication, I hope, speaks for itself.

Hubert Chapman
Brundall, Norfolk, 1996

The road to the school from the Weir, Botolph Claydon, to the Cross Tree as it used to be. East Claydon village school lay and still lies beyond, about half a mile on the left-hand side of the road to East Claydon.
Photograph: Maynard Chapman.

Schooldays at East Claydon
1906–1915

I was eager to go to school. My play-mate, Harry Wiggins, was there already and Vilona, who lived next door to me and was my elder by a few days, was even now pacing beside her mother for enrolment, intent to be first even in that.

As we set out Mother said, 'It's your first day, so I shall be at the school-gate at twelve o'clock to bring you home for dinner. You can go back with Lona for the afternoon.'

It was straightforward going - first along the lane beside our Weir Pond to the Cross Tree where the real village began, then past Webbs' the village shop and Harry's father busy in his wheelwright's yard and next again, Harry's uncle 'Herb' who was shoeing a great cart-horse in his smithy. On we stepped and now, on the right, came the post office, exactly like the old leaning farmhouse which once it had been, and then opposite, my jolly Great-uncle John's 'Rose Cottage' - and which other home in the whole village had four stately fir trees standing in line before it? Great-uncle John who really was great, much like King Edward, looked up as we passed, smiled and gave us a wave, but prim Aunt Emily was not to be seen; I had told them that this was my important day. No more than a few paces now and we were passing the cobbled path rising to the familiar doorway of my Granny and Grampy Chapman. All was silent there this morning, so soon we had grand Botolph House in view, larger than anyone's needs according to my young eyes. Its spreading cedar cast a great shadow over our path. By this time Mrs Blindell and Lona were far ahead. On the same side next stood Jesse Carter's quaint cottage. Jesse built great hay, corn and straw ricks within yards of my home in Weir Lane. Next, after passing his tightly-clipped box hedge, we must pass Tompkins's smelly cattle yard and barns, where, at times, a short-horn bull might be seen and then, since the yard adjoined the boys' school playground, at last we reached the school. I knew its outline. Harry had brought me already to prospect it, for daily we enlarged our world.

It seemed that Lona and her mother were already inside, so Mother and I paused. As she peered doubtfully over the white wooden fencing at the gravelled play-space I took in the outside of the aged brick-and-tile building, noting again the forbidding windows, too high for any view of the outside world, and, high up, the weathered stone inset with its date '1847' readable, but dim.

The only entrance to be seen was by way of a cloakroom, cramped and full of clothes, which led us in a step or two to the threshold of a surprisingly wide, high room full of infant children sitting in pairs at their desks and, amongst them, Miss Wyatt, their teacher, small and slim and smiling, and pointing to chairs placed next to a wood and glass-panelled door set in a long high wooden screen which appeared to comprise the room's whole side wall.

Headmaster White, and goodness knew what besides, were behind the screen and Lona, I supposed, also was there being entered as a scholar. So Mother and I quietly sat while I eyed the nearer children, some of whom I knew and who were peeping at me, while silently busy in their heavy fixed desks. It appeared that each must copy in a shallow sand-tray, with the point of a finger, letter shapes drawn large in white chalk on the blackboard raised at the class's front, while Miss Wyatt and her helper moved among them to help and supervise. I judged that this would give me no trouble, but just as I reached to give Billy Newton a helping hand, because he had drawn his letter 'E' the wrong way round, the door opened and Mrs Blindell and Lona emerged and a loud echoing voice called, 'Next!'

'Come along, boy,' Mother said quietly, 'and say good morning to show your manners' and we passed through the screen to see, rising before us, row upon row of large boys and girls, sitting perfectly still, their arms tightly folded before them, and a young woman assistant standing straight and silent at the side while John Alfred White himself was sitting at his desk, facing the largest of the boys. Even sitting he appeared to me as a giant with a fearsome gingery moustache and bold, unsmiling blue eyes.

His strong pink fingers were drumming on the desk, so carefully I said, 'Good morning, sir,' and he, 'Hubert is it? Take a seat, Mrs Chapman. Shall we have the particulars, then?' And in no time at all I was entered in his book. Laying down his pen he drew me to him to point to that last entry and say, 'What does that say, young man?'

When I replied, 'Me, sir,' he smiled and said, 'On the ball, eh, Mrs Chapman?' which made Mother laugh.

'Too much sometimes,' she said – and what did they mean by that?

'Take him to Miss Wyatt,' he said, 'he'll settle in.'

Turning then he did not see what I, in utter amazement, did see, as Mother also opened wide her eyes in surprise – the boy I knew as Andy, Jesse Carter's big son, sitting near us and positioned behind much larger Jed Price. Andy was grinning cheekily as he bent forward, swiftly unfolded his arms to twirl, stoke and fondle his imaginary moustache and then swiftly again resumed his position, his face now blank. It was all done within a second or two. The teacher at the side had seen but she merely pursed her lips, as observers over the room gently smiled.

Quite unaware of this Mr White patted me on the head and rose to lead us to the door, my mother for the moment bemused and I stunned; for it had been revealed to me in a flash that school could be very different from my imaginings, with surprises and even alarms beyond sand-trays and book-learning. I was intensely relieved to be going to Miss Wyatt, who, I saw now, had Lona pondering over a sand-tray, as Mrs Blindell stood smiling in the doorway, waiting to accompany my Mother home.

The year was 1906 and the time of year was mid-September. Again the term-opening had been arranged to accommodate the Chairman of the Managers and his fellow farmers, who annually in later summer, required the help of the older pupils in the fields for getting in the harvest. School was re-commencing for them and could now begin for me. Lona and I were both four years of age – 'coming five next month', as the elders would say.

❋❋❋❋

I found our headmaster absolutely daunting. Awed by his height, I had seen also the gaze of his bold, blue eyes. He was best viewed from afar. I put my trust in the screen and the door that was firmly closed.

His school at that time had about one hundred and twenty children attending, the youngest of five years and the eldest those of thirteen and, one or two, of fourteen years, drawn from my hamlet of Botolph Claydon, the villages of East and Middle Claydon, the small grouping of houses at Verney Junction and the outlying farms and lone places. We lay on the undulating clay of the Vale of Aylesbury, north of the Chiltern Hills and so in a green countryside, with farmers' fields reaching almost to our doors.

With the help of Rose Bradley, daughter of the Verney family's coachman, the lady assistant I had seen, Mr White instructed all above infant age, while elderly Florence Vere Wyatt, a short, slim spinster lady, who was utterly dedicated to her work, took charge of all the beginners. She too had help, that of Miss Lucy, a 'supplementary' with no supportive paper qualifications but great willingness and the valuable knack of gently inducing effort. Therefore, the school-roll divided roughly equally between the two commands, which operated entirely separately. For this the building provided the two large rooms I had briefly entered. Both were echoing and high, reaching into the exposed rafters and apex of the roof. Laid down with the school's first building, the uneven floorboards were deeply worn and knotted. The air space beneath them engendered a drumming effect from any movement on them, apart from the noise of iron-tipped leather boots in contest with the iron of the fixed desks.

The classroom walls were painted a heavy brown to head-height and, above, a cream which had faded into nothingness. The courses of the brick-work were everywhere discernible, and, of course, all the windowsills were out of reach, and the lower panes frosted. The window sashes required a 'long-arm', a hooked pole, to be operated. It appeared that Mr White only could be trusted to use it.

The gravelled play-space my mother had frowned over sufficed for the older boys, who had the benefit of a great elm standing at the far end, an ancient tree bearing signs that its trunk and lower branches - because of a shininess of the bark - had for years challenged the venturesome to climbing and heaving-up. The girls and infants shared a fenced-in area at the rear of the building and beyond this brick-built toilets could be approached along weedy, fenced paths. The boys' arrangement was repellent - I faced it only under pressure. The girls' and infants' shared facility was much less worrying - motherly older girls were on hand. They were helpful also in the matter of the grazed knees common among infant beginners. Needless to say, we children accepted all this as normality - all 'school' must be something like this.

Miss Wyatt's capacity for order and careful teaching, much it by quite enjoyable rote, kept us steadily busy. Inevitably the iron of our boots often met that of our desks, but for all quiet work her precise instruction: 'Foot-one; foot-two' had them placed side-by-side on the wooden foot rail. She would have hush for long periods. Often my eyes left my sand-tray and bead-frame for counting in tens, my

Harbutt's plasticine or crayon drawing to regard the door in the screen, for I developed an apprehension about it which stayed with me for several weeks - I think I never saw again its other side.

What I imagined of the scenes there derived from sounds - heavy echoing noises from hob-nails on hollow-sounding floorboards and desk stanchions, a sudden shaking of the screen and, on occasion an awesome switching sound balanced by bursts of music from a powerful harmonium - for Schoolmaster White was also organist and choirmaster for the parish church. The frequent robust singing of hymn and chant led me to suppose that he was rearing and perfecting conscripted choristers and I had no wish to become one. I could not envisage volunteers. As to the switching sounds, most parents were at one with him, saying: 'White gives the young villains no more than they deserve to keep order and he learns 'em well as well', showing here that his English was not necessarily theirs. At this point I record that my Great-uncle John White was not related in any way to Mr White, the schoolmaster. This I made plain to all who would listen; for, of course, there was, and is, a streak of White-ness in me.

Miss Wyatt's quiet domain, demanding though she was, her quick smile and her hand-pat if you happened to excel and the fact that she never punished (for her to say that she was shocked at a small misdemeanour as she held your hand and fixed you with sad, grey eyes through her gold-rimmed spectacles was enough), all these things ensured that gradually the screen ceased to worry me. So I remember Mr White's presence in our room as occasional only - mainly, as I recall, for a noisy replenishment of our distant iron coke-stove - a towering figure dwarfing a quite tiny one.

Miss Wyatt's helper, Miss Lucy, was the young daughter of my Great-aunt Bessie Norman and was, I felt, a source of possible protection from the unknown. Also, she smelt very nice when she bent over you to help with the counting of your cardboard shillings and pence, or your French knitting when it was in a tangle. Round her high-necked lace blouse she wore a heart-shaped locket. I was puzzled, when I mentioned these attributes at home, to hear Mother say sharply: 'And very nice too.' Miss Wyatt failed here, although she did possess a reticule swinging from her waist-belt which would rattle round your ear when she came close. She had no shiny back-comb in her hair either - just thin hair pulled hard back. A silver watch was pinned high on the outside of her plain white blouse. She snapped its cover to with a faint, sharp sound when she enjoined absolute silence

Pupils and teachers of East Claydon School about 1906. To the left stands headmaster Mr John Alfred White and to the right his one assistant Miss Florence Vere Wyatt. The author, aged five, sits cross-legged at the end of the front row on the right with the other infants.

Photograph: Hubert Chapman

The old village school at East Claydon, built in 1847.

Photograph: Courtesy of East Claydon First School

throughout the room.

We infant boys regularly joined the older boys in their playground in order to be directed into school, morning and afternoon, so each afternoon we, too, could watch to judge if Mr White were lingering after his mid-day dinner for his house stood but a short distance off and his tall figure could be seen as he left. I learned then to call with the rest: '"Bossie's" coming. He's coming - get into line!' He had been nicknamed long since: many of the villagers also referred to him succinctly as '"Bossie" White - along at the school.' On his approach I was with the first in line, because he was then seen close-to with not a glimmer of a smile beneath the carefully brushed moustache, to me an immensely tall figure in a tailored suit and shiny black boots, wearing a bowler with curled side-brim such as our fathers wore on grand occasions. The silence as we stood in our rows was profound - not a boot moved in the gravel.

'Infants,' he would say and carefully then we would go by way of the cloakroom, often pungent with damp clothes, to join our girl companions. On a sharper word the 'Big Boys', the massive ones like Andy Carter and his tall classmate, Ben Harris, went with heavy tread and Bossie himself to join the 'Big Girls' in their long white pinafores, thick skirts, black stockings and button-boots, for whatever lay in store for them.

It was a routine I began to accommodate with ease. It was something to be numbered with the great, Bossie's own, noisy Big-uns, while also learning their language.

I progressed enough in Miss Wyatt's care to leave Miss Lucy and the younger children's play-learning behind me and to be promoted to a seat on the room's gallery, an erection of fixed long forms and desks on raked stepping, which put high-fliers literally on high, on show and in view. There we were Miss Wyatt's own, and there we must proceed to certainty in tables to twelve times twelve, learn to multiply and divide by awkward divisors, such as seven and nine, acquire surenees in 'carrying' and 'borrowing' and to recognise how long words could be broken up in order to read and spell them, while taking whole those unamenable to this. Our handwriting was long-hand, requiring careful hooks, loops and spacings - by the width of the little finger between the words - all fitted into the lines on one's own slate, kept in one's own slot, at one's own exact position at the long desk on high. And, of course, the ability to read aloud on sight, and without prompting or error, with 'good expression' and so and so on. Below us sat those as yet unqualified, the strugglers, who might, or might not, rise to our height. We regarded them with a quite deplorable smugness, which needed to be brought low, as suddenly and unexpectedly it was. Measles, knowing no distinctions among high or low, sought me out and took me and my pride to bed precisely when a fire at night destroyed the gallery, ending a usage of more than sixty years. When I returned with other wan companions the gallery had vanished and, worse, prestige was lost by our having missed the sensations of blackened wood, split slates and ashes. I sat puffed up no more; a groundling again, knowing how all the lately-elevated must feel when unfeelingly, unreasonably, or just accidentally, they are reduced.

But already there was an exciting diversion. Beyond the school, quite near, were the new village hall, library and games room and, on their far side, Tompkin's Field where fascinating things were happening. Men had placed wooden pegs in the turf, had stretched strings from peg to peg, then stripped the turf to dig trenches in a wide pattern to make the foundations of a new school. We watched in every moment of spare time. Slowly it would rise, the school in which I would spend the main part of my school days, where with older eyes I saw John Alfred White shrink, year by year, to comprehendable

Building the new model school at East Claydon. Lady Verney with the contractor Mr Cripps.

Photograph: Courtesy of Sir Ralph Verney and East Claydon First School

The author and his elder sister Eva in the garden of The Weir, aged six and three respectively. Photograph: Hubert Chapman

proportions.

When I was six years old we were led by our headmaster and teachers in a long procession to the laying of the foundation stone. Preparations had involved and engaged every household. Mothers had received allocations of cotton material, white and blue for boys' sailor blouses, white and pink for girls' frocks, new collars and bow ties and white pinafores for the oldest pupils - all supplied by Sir Edmund and Lady Margaret Verney, the far-seeing originators of the whole scheme, who were ready and waiting to have the big stone placed in the midst of a concourse such as the village had never seen before.

The windy March day was at eleven o'clock and Cripps, the Winslow builder, in a smart suit and hard, black hat, stood by his crane, his hand upon the chain, as Lady Margaret, smiling proudly and trowel in hand, spoke words which the wind took and swept clean away. No matter - a great cheer arose and then, to huge hand-clapping, Mr Cripps slowly and gently lowered the stone for her to spread the mortar below it and have it exactly placed. In clear sharp lettering it marked the day - 5 March 1909.

More cheers and clapping, and many smiles amongst the watchers, as then in acute anxiety, I stepped forward with five other chosen pupils, each to lay a brick next to the great stone with real mortar, helped by the builder's guiding hand and using the small trowels which were to be our very own from that day on. I have ever since claimed that my brick lies next to the stone on its northward side. From Sir Edmund there was a pat on the head for each of the three boys and from Lady Margaret a kiss for each girl the boys deciding at once that this was a sound ordering of a possibly difficult moment. Then all the people sang: 'Except the Lord build the house they labour in vain that build it . . .' all the verses, our headmaster and the Rector, the Reverend Arthur Gordon, leading with impressive power, as the gusty wind pushed at us and wafted our singing to and fro. Sir Edmund's white hair stood up proudly as he sang and I could see that Lady Margaret, more than equally proud-looking, was intent on singing every word right to the end. She was a small but very bright-eyed and forceful lady.

There were long speeches from important people I did not know and so more cheers and clapping, but at last all was over and soon after that we children were dancing 'Sir Roger de Coverley' in the village hall. All day we had felt strange in our special holiday clothes, but I expect we forgot them when we settled to a proper celebration

The author aged 92 pointing to the brick he laid as a boy beside the foundation stone of the new school on 5 March 1909.
Photograph: Gillian Spencer

East Claydon School as it is today. Photograph: Gillian Spencer

tea, in which there was no bread and butter at all.

Some time later, in high anticipation, we were led, again in procession, to our completed school standing in its country surroundings utterly unique in style, as it is to this day. Its surprising lightness and brightness, its newness and freshness filled us with awe. Our old building, a school no more and left forever, looked dejected and drab, even lost, and became sadly silent. Weeds grew tall in the gravel. Sometimes, in passing I though I could hear a door inside idly swinging and banging - perhaps the one in the screen?

The new school had three airy rooms, one for infants, a middle room and a larger room where Mr White would be. We were like colts in a meadow on the smooth, quiet wood-block floors; low windows allowed us to see passers-by on the road, the trees in Church Walk, the flowers in the wide front garden; long, low, wall-blackboards, complete with chalk trays, awaited our drawing and writing and summing upon them; radiators stood ready to keep us warm in the winter and each cloakroom had low wash-basins and shining taps; all the furniture was light and new and the walls were painted in light, fresh colours - chocolate and cream banished forever. In our infant room was an astonishment on which we gazed in wonder - a tall mural mosaic showing such ruddy, healthy and happy children as never were climbing eagerly through flowers and gay bushes up and up to the Temple of Knowledge. It was by Henry Holiday, a famous artist of the day and his name was at the bottom.

We had a stoep, as it was called, or veranda, at each end of the school for open-air lessons, smooth asphalt playgrounds and paths, swings for the girls and the novelty of a giant-stride for the boys. There were vegetable plots for the older boys' cultivation with a fruit plot for grafting, budding and propagation, a shrubbery with flowering trees and interesting, unusual bushes, and for Mr and Mrs White and their daughter, a separate school-house, in matching style, with its own large garden and front lawn. All this occupied a full acre of land 'designated for educational use for all time' - remarkable then and distinctive still.

I left Miss Wyatt, Miss Lucy and Henry Holiday's climbers quite soon for the next room, near again to the headmaster. In that Middle Room, excitingly purposeful in every way, I encountered 'standards' for the first time. I was to be at the bottom of these arrangements in Standard One. Our teacher, of both the two standards there, was Lily Chapman, a distant cousin of mine, who was as able as Miss Wyatt to

The mosaic mural by Henry Holiday (1839–1927) in the new East Claydon School. Henry Holiday, the eminent Victorian artist, was commissioned by the Verneys to design and make this wall mosaic with its allegory of children climbing to the Temple of Knowledge.

Photograph: Courtesy of East Claydon First School and Mr D. Wharf

keep us busy and happy too. So I thought little of the concerns beyond the screen which separated us, for, though folding, it was solid and had no door.

Each morning Mr White folded it smoothly back on its runners, even with a flourish, for an assembly of all the school's standards, an occasion which we called 'Hymns', though, of course, it had prayers in it also and often exhortations. We were daily made to see, as he accompanied our singing, that he was no ordinary church organist. He swayed as he played, he pumped importantly with his feet, forcing the harmonium to give its all, as he gazed aloft far above our heads – heavenwards, we thought. Leading us daily in 'Hymns' he reduced a little more in height and no longer towered, for I now had a good view of him and Miss Bradley in their realm.

With the screen pulled back again we could settle to a bliss with Miss Chapman which obliterated all thought of anything beyond it or outside it. It was the greatest wisdom to leave us to her. Hers was the happiest class I was in as a child. The model timber-camps we made, the Indian villages, the kraals, the igloos, with blessed plasticine, matchsticks, stones, cotton-wool, gum and our mothers' cast-off cardboard boxes; the simple historical scenes we acted; the drawings we did on the wall blackboards and the work-songs we sang – with all this, we nevertheless achieved a standard of work in the all-important three R's which a visiting inspector reported as 'altogether high'.

A special memory remains of the letterbox proposed and provided – to stand on the wide windowsill in order to receive letters from us to her, requests for information on general knowledge items not directly concerned with schoolwork. A selected 'postman', or 'post-lady', would clear the box for her at home time on Friday and on Monday morning her responses would be collected from the box for distribution and a session of reading and discussion. The construction on the postbox was my commission – a shoebox stood on end, with the correct welcoming mouth and hinged door at the back, painted the most glaring scarlet I could find with 'ER' in black above the slot. My first question? Well, I cudgelled and then wrote: 'Dear Miss, if I were all by myself and lost on the desert, people say I wouldn't walk straight to get off, but I would walk round in a great circle. Which way would I go round – right-hand way, or left-hand way? Yours sincerely.' She found a feasible answer, too.

Lily Chapman was never a handsome woman; she was neither tall nor short, neither plump nor thin, and was even then somewhat heavy in the face. But her hair had auburn tints in it and was bunched up and waved attractively. No detail escaped us, even the mole on her chin. No more than twenty years of age then, she exuded directness, patience, kindliness and enthusiasm; there was comfort in her voice all through the day. Her voice and warm dependability made her seem another 'Mrs Do-as-you-would-be Done-by' in Kingsley's 'Water Babies', which she read to us to end each school day.

So I recall the sudden blank heaviness which fell upon us one day when I had advanced to Standard Two – when we learned that she had been persuaded, in fact promoted, to go far from us to work in the students' practising school of the Bangor Normal Training College for Teachers in North Wales. On the day of her leaving there was a scene of quiet misery and a gift for each one of us, matching well what she knew of us. Mine was a great block of Harbutt's plasticine, because I had been the standby for camels, elephants, bears, log cabins.

It decided me to attempt at home, in a sad, desultory way, to make birds and animals in relief and from that to progress perhaps to become a famous sculptor, probably in wood, because she had said that it was exactly what I could do when once I mentioned it to her.

Into the horrid blank of 1909, or 1910, came a young student teacher who was at first highly suspicious of us. We had worked much in groups, often changing for different sorts of class work; we could talk together while working, discuss and speak up, which was fearsomely new then, but now we became completely desk-bound and fretting. And 'Doll' – the nickname swiftly and unfairly given – had advantages; her father was an important officer in the local police force and so we gave in, being in a minority of thirty-odd to one. We found after a while that she was a sound instructress in the old-fashioned, rigid, step-by-step way. Bossie sought to help in this abrupt change in our learning situation. Her arrival brought him directly to us to loom in close proximity for long, tense periods, to move among us and to examine our work. Sometimes he would stand in the open doorway, fingering his watch chain, then go silently away. At times I had him right beside me and once, as he bent over my desk to flip over the pages of my exercise book, I had to resist feeling his cloth for here we all were in our weekday attire while he was at ease in a Sunday suit of pale blue cloth with darker blue stripes, sharply pressed trousers and shiny cufflinks in his sleeves. By and by he visited us less and less frequently and Miss Sellars' efficiency soon steered me beyond the screen and into Standard Three and the Big

Room at last.

It was a wide room with generous windows on either side taking in two groups, Standards Three and Four, as one, in the care of Miss Rose Bradley, Bossie's long-time support, and the other, 'Bossie's Own' placed before his desk and the harmonium, comprised Standards Five, Six and a tiny Seven, with at times even a suggestion of an ex-Seven, the one or two bright members who had 'learned everything', that is to say all the simplicities required for passing the early-leaving examination, which would release them, primed for the world of work, at the age of thirteen years.

Rose Bradley was a gentle lady of middle years; like Lily Chapman she was fair to gingery with engaging freckles. Her dress followed the hour-glass fashion of the time - long skirt, blouse almost to the chin, a strong belt round the small waist. Her hair was done forward-rolled with a bun at the back like our mothers'. On winter days she and Bossie often sat side by side on the ridged hot water radiator discussing matters on which we could only guess, while all standards were put to silent work. Miss Bradley's might be set to a composition, perhaps say: 'An old Boot tells its Story' on two sides of paper, and Bossie's to necessary word-polishing on scrap paper. Never at a loss in this he would write tricky ones on the blackboard to be written in best handwriting, twenty times each, in preparation for a later test on them, e.g. disappoint, dissatisfy, assent, ascent, embarrass, harass, accompany, accommodation, siege and seize. The older observers found this vastly interesting leading to speculation about the physical corrugations that must surely accompany the beneficent warmth which the animated sitters were keeping from us, the infinitely more deserving toilers at our desks.

In unruffled fashion Rose Bradley coped well in sharing the room, for Bossie's style was flamboyant and interruptions were frequent from visiting county officials, inspectors, impressive visitors from afar and, a new departure, a school nurse. Nor must I omit the 'kiddy-catcher' of the searching eye, with his all-important notebook, wearing his bicycle clips to show that he was a wide-ranging man. His quarry would be older girls kept back by their mothers to help with younger siblings, and boys put to work before their official leaving date by hard-pressed parents needing 'every penny' as they would endeavour to explain to him. To this his answer was: 'It is the law, missis. Tell your man I shall be at the school Monday morning to see if the boy's in.'

The first medical inspections for state-school children were instituted at this time, hence the visiting nurse and on the wall behind Bossie's desk the chart for eye-testing. It was an important moment in national education – 'mens sana in corpore sano' at last. 'A healthy mind in a healthy body'. While we were still with Lily Chapman our whole class had been involved in a first manifestation of this new care when, with a throat infection about, we went in pairs to a uniformed nurse in the girls' cloakroom each to gargle a pink liquid – perhaps permanganate of potash? In my case it was a horrible, spluttering fiasco. I either vaporised it or swallowed it whole, while the patient nurse sighed saying: 'Don't take such a *deep breath.* All right, you've had enough, better go.' Next came the first visit of a school doctor, a jolly man with a curious name – Carruthers, 'foreign' we supposed. Next came pressure for home money for the purchase of toothbrushes with wooden handles. One or two girls came to school wearing steel-rimmed spectacles and the swift ones with toothbrushes smiled more than usual.

Occasionally the Big Room provided the sensation of a switching, when a boy would be required to 'walk' as Bossie raised his desk lid to feel and find the switch within. Both would then proceed to the boys' cloakroom for treatment of a different order. It involved a vague something called 'impudence' and one or two boys only. These tough spirits, who were not at all put down by it, often returned smiling; they regarded it as routine, and gave useful hints on ameliorations. Had the worrying sounds from behind the Old School's screen meant simply this? I saw that our headmaster had fallen into a pattern of behaviour seemingly meaningless. I saw also that I was not of the calibre to qualify and realised that Bossie was something of a puzzle on closer view.

Soon I was with him in Standard Five, sitting within touching distance of the harmonium, daily more used to the diversions. As I was possessed of a magpie-jackdaw memory for pretty well everything he put before us, he began to include me among his leading lights and I became relatively happy and comfortable. Cousin Bernard and Lona also were nearby to share a daring quiet smile with me when visitors were on hand and we had a close view of what we designated his airs and graces, especially liking his grand moments. He wrote on the blackboard in bold, sweeping style, continuously preened his moustache and seemed conscious that he was a fine figure of a man destined to work with those not of his choosing. He taught well in the rule-of-thumb, regimented, repetitive way of those days, every minute of the school-day properly accounted for. Apparently nothing outside this was expected of him, apart from his commitment to the rector's services, the organ and the choir.

In class he disliked what he called unwarranted and unnecessary smartness. For example, with the large Mercator world map before us, he would require one of us to step forward to point, say, to London and I see now the sudden frown as I sought for Ontario and again when, for Birmingham, Bernard crossed the Atlantic for Alabama. A deep frown then - we knew we must desist. What might happen with Bethlehem and the famous steel-works, also in America, and Bossie the rector's right-hand man? We learned like Agag to go delicately, for a Samuel was on hand.

We became almost completely bi-lingual. Ten marks out of ten for oral reading called for care and in class English was spoken pretty well as required. Outside with our peers we reverted to that which ensured pace and acceptability about the village. Much of it would be incomprehensible to the residents of today. My family certainly would not permit its extremes and it would raise Bossie's ire remarkably. Examples were: ender (yonder), fligged (fledged), cridget (child); the possessive 'mine' allowed us his'n, her'n, your'n, their'n; and 'Gissa sucker' was never misunderstood - 'Please give me one of your sweets'. Should Bossie hear any of this he would correct it with force saying: 'Will you never heave yourselves from the mire?' Even now I have no knowledge of his origins - he spoke as the grand folk did - the rector, the doctor, the important people who came to see our new school.

Some must have heaved ourselves for we passed through Standard Five and into Six by the time I was eleven or twelve years old. Seven and even ex-Seven came within striking distance. No physical movement was involved, although if you could achieve ex-Seven you and your peers would sit at the back of the class working mostly by private study methods, a dazzling situation much to be desired. This I achieved by 1914, when the Great War began, along with Lona Blindell and my cousin Bernard, another of the numerous Chapmans, and both of my own age.

For numeracy we had a monstrous Pendlebury's Arithmetic, Bossie's own copy with a huge red ink signature in it; English exercises in the parsing and analysis of sentences and paraphrasing - terrible work this last on good poetry, dictionaries in constant use.

And, at last, we suffered no more of the maddening 'reading round the class', its pace dictated by the slowest stumbler. Instead the silent absorption of the abridged classics in Bossie's cupboard - Dickens, Scott and George Eliot at their simplest but satisfying enough to the word-hungry for the moment. Also, in my case, came the silent composition of an epic, its title, 'Cedric the Saxon', inscribed before any other word was written. It ran to several swelling exercise books before our headmaster took it up, saying: 'May I?' to return it silently later, frowning a little: recently a much abridged 'Ivanhoe' had been slowly read round the class. I forget where I placed Cedric for his heroic death, probably alongside Hereward in a last stand in the Fens.

One afternoon at home time and within a few months of my fourteenth birthday, Bossie put his hand on my arm saying: 'Stay behind a minute.' When everyone had left he turned to place his arm round my shoulder, 'Now, young man,' he said, 'What do you want to be and do when you are grown up?' My answer was immediate: 'An architect, sir.' I had been ensnared by the newly discovered joys of mensuration. The desire to emulate Grinling Gibbons and Chantrey, the great wood-carvers, had long diminished. No - there were town halls, mansions, piers to be built, cathedrals and churches to be magnificently restored without delay. Sir George Gilbert Scott of Gawcott village, no more than a half-dozen miles away, had done such things comfortably enough.

'Ah'! J. A. White said, 'a long and expensive training for that, you know. Think about being an architect in another way and a way tremendously important, but more easily managed from a small village like ours. I think you would make a good teacher. You could *be* a builder, you see, of *young minds*. Think about it. Talk it over at home. I could put you in the way of it. Off you go, then - no need to hurry. Tell me in a day or two.'

The same must have been said to Lona and, thinking about it, we decided, all parents concurring. Thus, on 1 November, 1915, at fourteen years of age, we could enter the County's Rural Pupil Teachers Scheme, subject to our passing tests. The 'two good vaccination marks' derisorily deemed sufficient qualifications for helpers such as Miss Lucy were not enough for the scheme. Consequently, one morning, a very superior gentleman arrived at the school, the Chief Education Officer himself. His shining machine - motor-cycle and sidecar, parked at the school gate - was a wonder to all. Astonishingly like Rudyard Kipling, whose picture I had recently seen, even to the spectacles and the trimmed, dark moustache, he exchanged no word with the candidates, though swiftly looking us over, while loftily accepting a whole stick of pristine white chalk from our surprisingly deferential Bossie. With this, and a flourish of his coat-sleeve, he entered on the blackboard six arithmetical problems, answers to be handed in when completed, or abandoned. He then left, requiring an essay to be written on three sides of paper, saying that he would return in the afternoon for all results and to hear us read aloud. In mid-afternoon, standing directly before the Grand Presence, Lona and I prepared to reveal what Mr White and his school had done for us, only to be stopped after no more than three or four lines of print. 'That will do,' he said. He glanced at our papers proffered by Bossie, thrusting them back at him with the words: 'They'll do - they'll do.' Then apparently in continual haste, and still with no word to us, he departed. 'Passed - well done!', Bossie said, looking quite as relieved as we were to hear the motor-cycle brought to life and go. We were launched, Lona and I supposed, on a day of stupendous, widespread launchings.

We two ex-Sevens had been approved for a scheme now long superseded, a four-year apprenticeship (though called a bursary) devised to provide teaching staff thought adequate for elementary schools. It had at least one advantage, in that by the time the bursary had run out it could be known for certain whether there was a sincere commitment to teaching and a wish to go on. Some who left adopted very different ways of life - two whom I knew prospered in the new world of radio.

A distant lady supervisor of all the local pupil teachers would provide our schemes of work, and the list of text books needed, for passing the Preliminary Examination for the Certificate, that which had been known as the Queen's Scholarship and was needed for entry to a teachers' training college. The subjects studied would be limited to those decided upon for young people of our background - School Arithmetic, with no geometry or algebra; English Language, with plentiful Grammar; some suitable Literature; English History, from Saxon times to the mid-nineteenth century, or only a little nearer our own day; Geography by countries; Botany as the only science; Art, that is, drawing and watercolour painting and no second language, either ancient or modern. Increasingly we would stand before a whole class for hearing oral reading, dictation-work and the testing of tables; or we would engage in pushing along slow readers in small groups, as

Bossie gave guidance day by day. He would be our instructor for our own course work, giving one hour to us at the end of each school day, with continuous homework. The distant lady would set, send and mark termly tests and require us to travel to her school to face formal annual ones sitting with other pupil-teachers. We would continue to occupy seats at the back of Bossie's class as ex-Sevens, becoming daily a little more 'ex', when occupied on the course work.

J. A. White now revealed himself as a suddenly different mentor. We could not begin our course officially until we reached our fourteenth birthdays, but smilingly he said: 'Better make a start, don't you think?' He brought books from his own shelves and was pleased as we pounced upon the complete 'Mill on the Floss', for in class George Eliot, even 'Silas Marnier', had been severely abridged; then 'Dombey and Son', that, too, having shrunk in class, but now complete. Amazingly he brought us 'Under the Greenwood Tree', perhaps to show us that schoolmasters can be human or perhaps because we were not yet ready for such as tragic Tess and the Dorset mayor who sold his wife for cash? Who knows? Bret Harte touched me closely with 'The Luck of Roaring Camp' and then, excitingly for me, came Conan Doyle's 'Tales of the Ring and Camp' to be absorbed at home and the back of the class. Lona meanwhile enjoyed 'The History of Mr Polly'. He came to us saying: 'What shall we discuss? What has taken your fancy?', perching himself on the adjoining desk, 'Dombey and Murdstone alike, hm?' He seemed to be a different sort of man, capable of surprises.

At this time he set the entire school and much of the neighbourhood suddenly agog. Village folk usually assign everyone a slot in their community and the schoolmaster could easily fall into a neat, sometimes prosaic, one. Such had been Bossie's, I expect, hitherto - a step below the parson and the doctor, but sharing their aura and world. But here, now, was this same man transformed in overalls and goggles, in a cap turned back to front, actually emulating the Great Presence from County Hall in Aylesbury, raising dust and commotion in the village street on a contraption resembling a great tricycle, propelled by a device of explosive and blue smoke, that brought people to their front gates and doorways in disbelief and amazement - John Alfred White, schoolmaster, intent on being in the forefront of the motor age. Well - Schoolmaster Read of Steeple Claydon had recently passed through on an ordinary pedal-cycle assisted by a small motorised wheel, but this of White's was outdoing all. 'Put together most of it hisself, so I hear tell,' someone said, 'in a mucky old shed up in Aylesbury. Who would have thought it!' For all to see it worked, if noisily. Mrs White and daughter, so rarely seen, veiled and in long dust-coats, sat side-by-side on a double seat at the front and Bossie on a single seat behind them, driving manipulating, concentrating and perspiring a little, as any pioneer would. They were watched until dust and blue smoke obscured them as they headed for the slope leading down to Middle Claydon and beyond. 'Making for Steeple, I'll be bound,' another said, 'to show off to Read - if he doesn't blow up before ever he gets there!'

It was at this time too, in this memorable summer term, that Charlie, another Chapman cousin and one of whom I was proud because of his cheerful inventiveness and drawing skills, brought to school a small, beautiful, wooden model of a steam traction-engine, made and lovingly painted entirely by himself. We crowded to see it and Bossie's eyes too lit up as he scrutinised it closely, almost fondling it, saying: 'And this afternoon I will show *you* something.' That something was a scale model, in metal, of a railway locomotive, lettered L.N.E.R., a working model, placed carefully before us on a front desk. We gathered round to examine it in wonderment.

'Phew!' Charlie exclaimed, forgetting himself, 'you didn't, sir, did you, sir - make it?'

'Yes,' Bossie said, 'some years ago. I'm thinking of starting again.'

Breathing deeply, Charlie said: 'It's a 4-8-4.'

'It is a 4-8-4,' Bossie agree.

'Oh, sir!' we all breathed together, 'we never thought - not any of us—.'

'Thought what?' he asked, smiling broadly, giving the moustache a double twist.

'Well—' we said and then could find no suitable way to finish, our breaths taken clean away. Baffled I gazed at the pink hands in puzzlement, pink but strong.

Cousin Charlie displayed an early knowledge of mechanical things. He and I were given scope on the long wall blackboard to portray spreading scenes which usually came to be railway trains at speed. We established, for a time, a monopoly in 'Engineering Wonders of the World' by taking turns in borrowing the glossy volume from the children's room in the village library. In it we bored the Alps, bridged the Bristol Avon, built the Eddystone Lighthouse, skirted precipices beneath snow-sheds in the Rocky Mountains in Canada and tossed around words like 'funicular', 'thrust', 'head-of-steam', 'turntable', 'cow-catcher'. On the wide expanse of blackboard Charlie provided the onset of steam and smoke, locomotives, carriages, trucks, tracks and signal-gantries with accuracy, while I put in the aqueducts, tunnel-ends, hills and valleys and general background scenery.

We were often put to this task when visitors were expected. They were frequent, for East Claydon County Mixed School was becoming widely known as a model village school. It was useful for the drawing to go on during visitations; so there would be Charlie concentrating best with his head on one side and tongue in and out, while adding L.N.W.R. to a saddle-back tanker and whispering: 'Make the most of this, eh? Bossie likes showing us off. Look how he's talking and smiling.'

We now awarded him full points in most of his activities. Work and class arrangements went smoothly day-by-day, and it is noteworthy that Mick and Jim were no longer required to 'walk'. They had volunteered to clean and polish the tri-car regularly in their own time, for Bossie to say no, they should do it in school time; so they made such a shining job of it in his new shed, that he insisted on payment – lemonade, cake, biscuits tendered by Mrs White herself at her back door.

And I have a clear recollection that at this time too he might be seen in the boys' playground, at morning or afternoon break, helping the striders to circumnavigate their giant-stride. With the help of his height and a push at a boy's seat, he could propel him to the full extent of his rope into the most satisfying upward curving leaps, eliciting cried of: 'Me next, sir!' – 'Hold tight, Harry, you're flying.' – 'Make me fly, please, sir!' With Harry grounded Bossie then stood flushed, with arms akimbo, boys pressing to him, as he said: 'You grip the rope hard and run as hard as you can before you leap – that's the secret.'

One summer afternoon he came to us ex-Sevens, who sat gazing almost longingly at the open windows while idly turning the leaves of our books, 'as if next week would do,' as my mother would say, saying to Bernard and me: 'Fancy a change of scene? My lawn needs a trim – the machine is ready there and oiled.' 'Oh, yes please, sir,' we said and we were away on our first recruitment and the prospect of a full hour in the open air in school time. Having taken turns with the machine, shorn about half of his daisies, we stood considering a swift dash along Bossie's garden path to assess his raspberry canes, when, before either had moved on the suspect thought, Bossie himself appeared, carrying fat ripe strawberries on a large cabbage leaf: 'Half-time!' he said, 'sit yourselves down in some shade while you deal with these. Well done so far, but I mustn't stay.'

He left us as we chose a lilac bush for shade and sat to savour the gift, far from conscience-free.

'Fancy Bossie doing this,' I said. 'Did we thank him? I *think* we did.'

Clearly, a schoolmaster could live in two worlds and suddenly become a scatterer of our pre-conceived notions, even well-established ones. Another memory of 'Bossie' White directly concerns me. I was reading in a quiet period when he came to place on my desk a large watch in a gun-metal case. It was motionless and its milled winder was missing, that part which when depressed would also adjust the hands. 'Perfectly sound,' he said, 'in working order, except that the winder is lost. Borrow it to see if you can bring it to life again.' The winder must have been squared at the insertion end, because the small hole into which it must fit was square. I must think and think again. I remember well his laugh at my solution. My winder was a horse shoe nail, squared in its length as such nails are, but cut off by Harry's Uncle Herb, the farrier, at the correct point of size of fit the small square hole. The watch lay ticking away as if to recover lost time. 'Let me try – let me try,' Bossie said. 'If it truly works it shall be yours.' He inserted the nail, which I had attached to a leather shoelace against loss. It worked and, for the first time in my life, I was the owner of a watch.

The Great War of 1914–18 began in my twelfth year and continued through my thirteenth with little impact at first on the village, although as early as September, 1914, one Claydon man had lost his life in northern France. He was an Old Contemptible and so a volunteer, as were all British forces at first sent to confront the German armies. There was a sort of sad pride in him about the village but as yet no worrying apprehension about others. A family of Belgian refugees were being cared by Slades of the post office, where language was a double difficulty in understanding fully how they could be in a strange land and so far from home. In a humble way I was able to help in Webb's shop one day. I could explain that the Belgian lady wished to buy *bread*. and was not suffering from any sudden pang, or pain, on which Miss Webb said sharply: 'Well, why didn't she say so anybody can understand? You had better come behind the counter when these

Belgiums walk in' – this with a small touch of sarcasm.

The German Kaiser, Big Willie and his son, Little Willie, were regarded as comic characters (as in a bizarre way they were) who would fail utterly, as in the end they did. Besides, we had Kitchener and French to assure it. We older boys made careful drawings of them and the leaders of the Allies, which Bossie pinned to the school notice-board and daily he brought in his newspaper to display the Western Front, a wavy black line stretching from the English Channel to Switzerland.

After morning 'Hymns' we learned and sang the national anthems of the nations who were our allies to date. The Belgian anthem, of course, was the first to confront us and I hear still the opening as we sang it – 'Fled the years of ser-er-ervile sha-a-ame, Belgi-um 'tis thine hour at last—' and Bossie's cry of: 'Stop for goodness sake!' – then his frowning return to the keys and his fierce foot-pumping to try again with 'Belgium *'tis* thine hour', deciding that this it must be. The war was still remote and almost unreal as the summer term of 1915 ended and the long summer holiday began.

In the middle of the holiday, while I was working in the hay field, we two prospective Pupil Teachers suffered a shock. Bossie left our school for a larger one in the Chiltern Hills and there would be an unknown successor to take us and the school in hand in September. From the shores of Essex he would come – a sea-faring man? Lona and I conferred and were utterly at a loss. We had been given no hint beforehand, except, perhaps, minor ones. On the last day of term he had given me his red ink inscribed Pendlebury and Lona a surprise volume from his shelves. We concluded that the ways of headmasters are incalculable and strange and worriedly pondered on the newcomer. The Chairman of the School Governors let it be known in the village that he was a lively little fellow – little? – and that in his opinion the committee had chosen the right man. Inescapably, from the first day of November, we must commence our bursaries and work for and with him towards the examination of 1919. How now would it be managed?

I saw John Alfred White only once more. When I was aged about seventeen years and in the final year of the bursary, poring over a case of ammonites in the County Museum in Aylesbury, I felt an arm round my shoulder just as in the school-room at East Claydon three years before. I at once stood up: 'Oh! – Mr White,' I said, checking in good time the 'Bossie' which could so easily have escaped me.

'I didn't recognise you at first,' he said. 'Ah, yes - I see, ammonites from the Calvert clay pits. Up tails all - hey? But leave them for a bit. Come and have coffee and talk.'

It became a long man-to-man exchange. He looked much the same, moustache exactly as of old, and now was flaunting a beautiful silk neck-scarf. I was considerably taller and was not noticeably prosperous on my fledgeling teacher's pay. Claydon people, my own folk, his school in the Chilterns (quite unlike Claydon's) my hopes for the future, and emerging plans occupies us while several coffees cooled, or went cold, until he suddenly took out his pocket-watch, to say that he must go: 'Ladies, you see,' he said, 'must not be kept waiting. Mrs White will have finished her shopping tour. Now why did I go to the museum - you have made me forget.' I had meant lightly to ask him if internal combustion had brought them to town and in what shape of vehicle, but the opportunity was lost as he took my hand to say: '"Bossie" - that was it, wasn't it - "*Bossie*"? I knew you all called me that - oh, yes. And as for you, never forget I told you that you would make a teacher. Prove me right and then come to see me one day.' Then, smiling, he left me.

I watched the tall straight figure as he strode across the Market Square until he was gone and stood thinking I know not how long. Moments with him long past came crowding in and regrets, too, because when I had become of of his 'top ones' I quite soon discovered a wish to know him more fully. But he left, as people say, 'for pastures new' and I never saw him again.

I know I owe him much. I am sure he managed my first schooling in that old building of the last century as well as it could be managed and it was under him in the new that I came to know what I wanted to do in life. While in the care of dedicated Florence Vere Wyatt and then of inspired young Lily Chapman, whom he wisely trusted to go their own ways about us, unconsciously, I suppose, I came to understand how learning, teaching and growing up were best done. His responsibilities for me spanned almost nine years of my early life, yet he remains to this day a tantalising enigma.

Pupil Teaching at East Claydon School 1915–1916

Two unrelated circumstances brought a strikingly different headmaster to East Claydon School. By the year 1915 the roll of pupils had fallen permanently below the one-hundred line, threatening a reduction of A. J. White's salary. A posting to another larger school in the Chiltern Hills probably satisfactorily enhanced it. The East Claydon Managers took swift advantage of the other circumstances, even as the prospective pupil-teachers conferred on what appeared to be a dismaying desertion.

War can be ridiculous as often as it is horrendous and it had brought senseless sporadic enemy shelling to non-combatants on the shores of Essex, where A. C. Walter was headmaster of a village school in what had become a danger-zone. He joined the Royal Naval Voluntary Reserve and decided that, for the safety of Mrs Walter and their small daughter, aged only a few months, he must move inland without delay. Prescience must be credited to the Claydon Managers, who might have been tempted to take 'Bossie' White as a pattern. They must have seen in this applicant, so very unlike him, one who, as the Chairman said, would 'get things moving pretty fast' and their prescience was soon borne out.

On school opening in September no one eyed the newcomer more closely than the two Pupil Teachers to-be. Before us was a spare figure, certainly not little, except for our mental comparison with his predecessor, a tense man having a brisk air of command which pulled everyone up to a fixed straightness. He was sober in dress with no attempt at style, his face lean and pale, his gaze direct and all-seeing – a twirled moustache was quite unthinkable. His hair was raven-black and only just controllable. Yet, around the eyes, deep wrinkles promised a readiness for laughter, although nothing near it was shown in school that first day, nor for some days to come in a two-sided period of summing-up. It was plain that height and bulk need be no measure of command.

At morning break, he sought out Vilona and me to say: 'Ah-ha, young people. We must get together, don't you think? Mrs Walter wants to meet you too. Shall we say a few minutes after school this afternoon? Come to the house.' *Come to the house?* - this was astonishing and, furthermore, I still have no recollection at all of Mrs White as a person. We knew already that Mrs Walter was a qualified teacher herself. At four o'clock we were introduced to a kindly, gentle lady who welcomed us in saying that we must meet at once 'Number One in the Household' as Mr Walter introduced her, their smiling golden-haired daughter aged, as I have said, a few months only. Having proved acceptable to her, we were then led to the room which was to be 'the Den', waiting to be organised. 'You could get all these books sorted for me,' he said, 'and put in order in the shelves. Also catalogue them - would you?'

'Oh, yes,' we breathed, and he continued: 'Of course, read any and every one you fancy, because this is where we shall settle most days after school, come November One - the great day!' It became a moment of rising excitement and wonder that our doubts could be dispelled so swiftly. We hurried back to our homes starry-eyed, to acquaint our parents of vistas unimagined, yet right before us, ready, even waiting.

'Steady on,' my father said, 'early days.'

Meanwhile we took our places in class with the older pupils to experience teaching of a vigour and ingenuity beyond anything we had ever seen in the Big Room - much swift sketching on the blackboard, hand-made colour charts brought 'to make this clear' and then 'to make that plain' and now 'come forth in my place, Molly, to prove it'. Bernard and I were set to plan, make and place an attractive time-chart round the wall spaces of the room. 'Better begin with the Romans, though there were a jolly good many people around here before that pushing crowd came on the scene.' Miss Bradley quietly watched in wonderment. Inevitably she and hers were included, or were drawn in. Again my father said: 'Steady on. It's a good thing this man is not the build of White, or the whole framework of the building would require strengthening.' My mother just said: 'Hm!' on that *rising* note which indicates pleasing expectations. After every school day there was more to be told.

The village became quickly aware of him. His strong voice, of attractive timbre, could be heard well beyond the confines of the school. Passers-by paused as we land-lubbers were shown how we should sing. Also, useful scraps of geographical, historical, mathematical and other information could be picked up from the road when our windows were opened on a still afternoon. The harmonium, from having been elevated to organ status, now stood silent for long periods, its keys untouched.

'We have our voices, haven't we?' our new mentor said, 'and this,' giving his tuning-fork a smart tap on the instrument's wood to bring forth its sweet middle-C.

'With this,' he said, 'we have anchorage wherever we are. Hum that note - now, slowly, open your mouths. That's our platform.'

So we stumbled into part-singing, puzzling my mother. Is it '*Sleep, sleep, beauty bright*' which you are trying to sing? It's a curious tune - are you sure you have it right?' and to this, in high conceit, I replied: 'It's the *alto* part - we have to be able to sing both parts.'

'At the same time,' Father asked, laughing. 'What a man you have there!'

'*No*,' I would say, exasperated.

Relegated to our deepest cranial recesses were the songs in the well-thumbed Song Book for Schools, resting idle now in the classroom cupboard, songs such as '*Some Folks do*' - slightly rumbustious and so our favourite - '*On the banks of Allan Water*' - Miss Bradley's favourite for its heavy poignancy - also, of course, '*Three Cheers for the Red, White and Blue*' and '*In Happy Moments Day by Day*', which we had often requested in order, as we whispered together, 'to see Bossie go all dreamy'. These had been sung in unison, the harmonium leading, and almost certainly had been sung by our parents before us long ago in the old school.

'Yes, there are some good old songs there,' A. C.Walter agreed with Miss Bradley - We thought amongst ourselves that she was missing '*Allan Water*' - 'We will take a look at one or two of them some time. Meanwhile, something fresh and new, I think.' And turning to us: 'What shall we begin with? "*Ah, shall it ere be*"—? You really gave your best to it yesterday. Now there *is* a melody for Miss Bradley. A good, deep breath then. Take the note and all sing alto and I will sing the lead. Be ready to change over after, and after that again we will divide up and see how we like it that way.' It was the first time that I, or any of us, had met that wonderfully built, even haunting, Thuringian Air: it has stayed with me ever since. After something like that he would say: 'Well done - all sit now and just listen, I've something for you that you will long to learn and to know to the last note' and from a ping of his fork his voice would will the room, with:

'Come sing, come sing of the Great Sea King
And tell of the days he rode in,
For he rides at the head of the Mighty Dead
At the red right-hand of Odin –
As the red right-hand of Odin' – all the verses and then a grin and a wait as we sat lost in the vivid pictures in the song, lost in the power of what we had heard from so slight a man.

'They could sing as well as fight, those Norsemen,' said he when he finished. 'They had salt sea air in their lungs. Now, Bernard, where are you going to place these Norsemen on your time-line?'

His vigour outside school brought comment, even incredulity – a schoolmaster to be seen digging in his garden two hours before morning school and most evenings? 'Doing John Gamble out of his bit of extra pay, that is. Old John gardened for White for years,' one said when the matter was brought up. On Saturday mornings the schoolmaster and larger boys, like Mick and Jim, were to be seen almost frenetically re-ordering the school's large front garden and – would you believe it – by a paper plan pinned to a post. Nor was Mrs Walter absent from the scene. Fortification was her role, with lemonade and cake. 'Boys require regular fortification,' A. C. Walter declared. John Gamble, who did general outside tidying as one of his duties as janitor, had a first-hand view of these things and in perturbed fashion grumbled: 'You hardly know where to turn for him, first here, now there, next gone. Mr Gamble, he says, *Mister* – never had a Mister from White – Mr Gamble, he says, what's to be done with this wilderness? – meaning the shrubbery. Shrubbery? I says. Best left alone, says I, but he's gone before you can get another word out. Next day it's where can he get pergles, or some word like that, for his missis's roses to climb up. Pergles? I says, do you mean poles? Why, Sam Whiting, Steeple Claydon and then he's off again afore I can get to know what he's got in mind for this pergle, whatever 'tis.' He informed all who would listen about the latest 'how-do-you-do up at the school'. No man better at dispensing general information, he gave the insistent impression that he was working amidst continuous earth tremors. However, Mrs Esther Chapman, as permanent as the brickwork, who kept 'the inside' spotless and our desks highly, even squeakily, polished, observed in her thoughtful way as she walked home when her chores were done, that no-one could expect things to stay the same anywhere. The family had been in the war already and 'he', she was told, was a navy man. 'And it's nice to see the house lived-in - if you see what I mean,' she added. 'A man for a bit of humour', it was noted in the Post Office and Webbs' General Store, but our people were guarded about that in newcomers. It was conceded that he meant no harm by it. Also, if a little gossip was being relished by the regulars it was seen that he just smiled and might raise an eyebrow - nothing more; so 'a man friendly to all, ready to fit in and what', they said, 'can be wrong with that, since the young-'uns seem to like him?'

We who had a close, clear view from our desks often sat wondering what he would do, or require of us, next, in order, as he said, smilingly, to stir our brains, to get us moving. Most mornings when we took our places his blackboard greeted us with a small mental exercise, e.g. 'What is the 23rd letter of the alphabet?' As we sat frowning and scratching our heads he would say, 'Only a second to find it the easy way, who is going to be first? He had found in us what he decided was an inland lethargy overlaying potentialities which required shaking up. His dynamism would have pointed to the same need in many rural communities at that time.

Although the Great War was a full year on he did not refer to it in school. He knew that it would beckon him soon. We did not know then that he was 'RNVR'. The wavy black line of the newspapers, which Bossie White told us was the Western Front, stayed in almost the same position month after month, as Claydon learned that chirpy Harry Tomes of East Claydon and young Slade of the Post Office family, where the Belgian family was staying - the one whom the village cricket eleven could ill spare - were two men who would never return.

We sang the national anthems no more, except our own in two parts - our allies had become too numerous. Instead we often asked for 'Eternal Father, strong to save', because his alto, as we sang, was so moving. He seemed to be looking not at us, nor anything around us, but to be gazing far out over a multitude of waters. Also, we knew that Charlie Whitmarsh, one of Bossie's tough older pupils, was somewhere on those waters on his mine-sweeper called 'The Jackdaw'. He had looked in on us on leave, all smiles, and we present older ones had written letters to him. We thought of Charlie as we sang, because, so far, we had received no replies.

Action for Lona and me was not long delayed. 'Foreman, step forward,' the command came and I was made leader of the boys on the garden plots, on digging post holes for the erection of pergolas, Sam Whiting of Steeple Claydon having found some seasoned ash; next on the making of wooden hanging baskets for the verandahs - 'for the flowers that bloom in the spring, tra-la,' he sang, while doing the hanging himself. 'And me for the watering of 'em, no doubt - up steps,' John Gamble privately grumbled.

We were sent on precise expeditions, one to the spinney beside the village recreation ground, there to identify the mixture of standing trees and place them in a ground plan; another to name and record every shrub, wild flower, herb and grass in a stretch of field-hedge which the Chairman-farmer planned to lay in the winter, our best results to be presented to him at the next managers' meeting and all to be accomplished in prescribed time, so no dallying - 'or better still,' A. C. Walter suggested, 'make him a book with all your findings done in colour, Master Hubert to design the cover.'

Lona took older girls to cookery classes in the Old School, was put to egging-on slow readers in small groups and was made forewoman-instructress in Miss Sellars' needlework lessons, where she was put in charge of the running supplies. Even now she would recall the urgent small cries of 'Forty-cotton, please' - 'Tacking-thread, please' - 'Joining-off wanted', this last a colloquialism still a mystery to me. As to direct teaching, 'Not yet,' A. C. Walter said, 'Learn by watching for a while. You can set some dictation now and again and there will always be slow readers needing you. Especially note how Miss Bradley quietly and smoothly changes lessons.'

Next, two afternoons each week, for an hour after school, Mrs Walter would give us piano lessons free of charge on her own piano. 'Always useful,' she said, though at fourteen years we would be beginning late. 'Never mind - fun as well,' she said. I blush to think of my solitary practice sessions on Miss Wyatt's small harmonium in her echoing infants' room after school, such was my eagerness to get at a keyboard. I was awed at being allowed to touch the worn, yellow keys and puzzled that my foot-pumping was always gusty and asthmatic, nothing like her smooth flow had been. My scales, exercises and 'Nelly Bly' announced distresses I hoped no-one would hear, though John Gamble did once look in to say: 'Try to leave that instrument how you found it. I thought I heard it shouting for help.'

Lona left me far behind in facility on the keys. That was proved beyond any doubt when, after a while, Mrs Walter put us to a duet entitled 'Qui Vive!' in preparation for a hair-raising affair, for me, on the concert platform in the village hall. Tactfully, she assigned Lona to the 'Vive' and me to the left-hand-side thumping. In the concert speed was the saving grace for me, as was Lona's brilliant cover. I am sure she became valuable in her schools as I, in this way, was not. The only excuses I could muster for my limitations on the keys were that long handling of field and garden tools had forever stiffened me. I am always grateful to A. C. Walter's gentle 'Maudie' for her patience with me, for she led me humbly to honour in these later years the Young Musicians of the Year every year.

'November One' duly came for the official Pupil Teacher Scheme to begin, but A. C. Walter had well anticipated it. It would be as Mr White had informed us, but now this quite different instructor and guide would take us in hand, indeed into his own Den, which we ourselves had helped to prepare. We would receive payment from the County, our contracts laid it down, of two shillings and six pence per week in the first years of the bursary, rising to seven shillings and six pence in the fourth. Our distant supervisor now sent by post trial test papers, which were returned to us spread with red ink comment, which, I suppose, was helpful to A. C. Walter, while suitably sobering to us. She would supervise all the subjects of study. As they did not have the range of her Wolverton Grammar schools syllabus I suppose that she found the extra commitment manageable. We now bought all the recommended text books. At this point A. C. Walter said: 'Not good enough. You must have Latin, Algebra and Geometry as well and we will start these at once,' and we did. Little came of it through the disturbances of the war, but he gave me the spur to follow them as best I could, mostly alone.

Our bursaries had scarcely begun when he engaged in a scheme not laid down, arising from our immediate reading right through, of the prescribed '*Merchant of Venice*'. So, in the Den it was: 'Lona read all the ladies' parts, please, Hubert all the men, except Shylock – I claim Shylock.' He sensed our puzzlement at the immediacy but would say only, and mysteriously, 'Patience, patience, my children. December will reveal all.'

A few days before Christmas, in a London all lit up and seen for the first time, and in a state of continuous wonderment, we had Dover Wilson's text astoundingly enlivened for the three of us by Lilian

Braithwaite, Matheson Lang and Henry Ainley in person on the stage, in matinée, of the St. James's Theatre. For this we were conveyed from the sleepiness of our Claydon lanes by way of steam train to Baker Street Station and then, in a huge confusion of traffic, to the plush and gilt grandeur of that old theatre, there to feel the utter reality and then the solemnity of sitting in the grand dress-circle and to gaze in awe at the velvet and gold of the majestic curtains masking the stage, growing more excited with every moment at the glittering concourse gathering around us and the orchestra's urgent promise.

I feel again the stir within me as the curtains silently parted to take us to Italy, far in place and time, where were three young men extravagantly garbed in velvet, the grandest Antonio who, before the play was out, would be within a hair's breadth of death; then to Portia and her maid in her grand home in Belmont, where later her choice of a husband would be made; but then back to 'A Public Place' and there Bassanio, Antonio's friend, who is negotiating with Shylock the fateful loan, because Antonio himself will be coming in a moment to put himself in fearful jeopardy thereby.

But, for the moment, Bassanio is pressing and Shylock is delaying: 'Three thousand ducats - well?' and then Bassanio, pressing again: 'Ay, sir - for three months' and again Shylock: 'For three months - well?' We knew it all, Lona and I sat stock-still. For me it was an early, compelling understanding that Shakespeare was of the stage, not, first of the study or even of A. C. Walter's Den, although the theatre shows continually how much of a scholar also he was.

When it was all done we rode on the upper deck of an open-top bus along Regent Street, dazzled by its maze of Christmas lighting, the darkness having long fallen, to the busyness of Baker Street Station again to head for home on the 'long train' into Metroland. Had our guide said as we climbed our hill, under the stars, to a village seemingly quite asleep - as he may well have done: 'What do you remember best of all this day's doings?' we would have replied together, I know: 'Everything - forever.' We had, in fact, discussed little in our prolonged state of astonishment. He understood and as we parted, to return to our homes, he simply said: 'We must do more of this, Stratford-upon-Avon perhaps - the Memorial Theatre,' though the war very firmly precluded that.

Shakespeare should be lifted from the page - that was it, and it must be done while still he had time to do it.

Quite soon, instead of the hour of course work one afternoon, we must repair to the Den, he said: 'For something different. Just bring yourselves – your two listening selves.' Wondering, we went to settle into armchairs, firelight flickering over us and the semi-order of the room, puzzled because no word of explanation had been given, nor was any given now. 'For something different,' he said again as he lit the oil lamp positioned on the desk behind him. It cast a glow on a thick volume at his elbow. I discerned '*The Rise and Fall of the Dutch Republic*' – J. L. Morley, three inches thick and something I must read some day? He took up the book beside it. 'David Copperfield,' he said and I could see that he had it three parts open. 'This is the full edition,' he continued 'all the difference in the world from the school edition. This is Chapter fifty-three. May I just read it to you, straight through?'

'Yes, please,' we said together.

'Right then,' he said and began in a quiet even voice, never changing tone, lifting from the pages the reality of what could happen all too easily to young life in 1850, when Charles Dickens himself was a young man. For Dora, who had been Spenlow, had not wished for her David, her very dear 'Doady', to be with her upstairs at the last – much, much better not. Just the good, dear Agnes, please, and he to be near, but in the parlour below, caring for her small friend, Jip, who also was so very poorly. I was overwhelmed. The school Dickens had said nothing of all this. We sat fearfully silent, dread growing every moment, with every word. We knew that feeling well – each week now in the village reading-room's copy of the Illustrated London News were full pages of photographs of smart officers who had 'made the Great Sacrifice' in France, on and under the sea, and how many unpictured other ranks, or ordinary seamen, like Charlie Whitmarsh – how many? And had not worried Thorpe, the postman, brought desolation already to homes we knew? Dread was all around – we sat rigidly still. Loving, innocent Dora, who had been 'brought up spoiled', as Claydon would explain it, had come, too late, to know self-revelation and to express it, was dead and forever still.

As he closed the book on the last words of that fraught chapter, he looked across at us both, saying: 'Do every great writer full justice by reading his every word. Make it your business to know as thoroughly as you can the times in which the words were written. Avoid abridgement like the plague. Home and tea now?' Our thanks were poor to the point of incoherence. We went home to our teas, wordless.

St. James's Theatre and Shakespeare there, and now this, were done, I am certain, because of urgency, that before the navy called him he must put these two young people, standing on an increasingly uncertain professional threshold, to some real thinking without waste of time, that soon he would be gone and then who would do it?

Fund-raising in the village was necessary for the purchase of wool, khaki and navy-blue, to maintain supplies for the busy home-knitters meeting regularly in the village hall, for the daily increasing needs of the Red Cross and for sustaining Belgian refugees. We had the inspiration of Florence Nightingale herself. She had spent many of her last years at Claydon House, because she had been the sister of the late Lady Parthenope Verney, and as a little old lady in a shawl and lace cap, looking much like the aged Queen Victoria, she looked down from a small photo frame in the village reading room. Thoughts of what she had stood for, had done and endured where there had been terribly frightening need, far from home, came crowding in as the work went on. Socials and concerts were organised to bring in funds and purchasing power. All talent was welcomed, or impressed, or cajoled, and A. C. Walter was soon drawn in to sing.

'What shall it be?' he pondered, the laughter wrinkles deeply creasing, '*Nirvana*, do you think?, or *Mair, my Girl*, something soulful? No - I've got it, *Dinah, beautiful Dinah*, that's what it shall be.'

When it came to Dinah on the concert platform in the crowded hall, his voice ringing with certainty in its power, his personal delight in the song obvious all through and his 'Maudie' smiling and nodding as she played for him, I felt I had a proprietary interest in both of them. All but the chorus of the old song now eludes me. That it brimmed with affection the engaging refrain clearly shows: '*Dinah, beautiful Dinah, you are the gal I love best – Dinah, no-one looks finer when in her Sunday best dressed – Peep dear, peep from your winder, gaze on your lover-boy true, whose heart is burnt to a tinder and all for his love, dear, for you.*'

On the rapturous conclusion one of our elderly matrons was heard to say: 'Fancy a schoolmaster singing a song like that! Still, his heart was in it - anybody could see that - different from Bossie White by a long chalk.'

'Well,' said her companion, 'White had his music, too. I sung for him in the Church Choir for years, now didn't I?'

'Different though,' said the first, 'the music, I mean, and the men.' The prolonged encores brought forth *Stone-Cracker John* for more encores, applause and urging whistles from the young blades standing far back, but immediately it was over he stepped down and made his way to me, saying: 'Come on - get your coat on. Leave them to it. Mrs Walter will be tied to the piano for another half-hour. I must have some air,' and he and I left for a long walk through the village in the keen night air and a tense discussion on 'this damnable war' and how could the world ever recover from its madness - as well as what I might be doing in the years ahead which was far from clear, and then what would be required of him very shortly, because the fighting nations were interlocked and he was on early call for the navy. We were then well in to the year 1916, with no end to the conflicts within sight.

The call came with blinding suddenness at Easter and he was gone. The two Pupil Teachers were confronted by instant blackness and loss in which we learned that Mrs Walter would take charge of the school and that 'other arrangements' would be made for us, which is where J. T. Read, my next, and third, village headmaster would come in. I went to Mrs Walter to say in stumbling fashion that anything I could do to help her and small Edith I would do without fail - garden, errands, anything, please let me. She was wan and taut and said: 'Yes, please, do. Arthur said it is exactly what you would do,' but she could say no more and I went home with feet like lead.

The arrangements were that Lona and I would pass to the care of John Thomas Read, of Steeple Claydon School, for the continuation of our bursaries, that larger village being three miles away and almost unknown to us. We would go on the first day of June, using our own means of getting there, my father, less than comfortingly, saying: 'Looks like Shanks's pony.' Meanwhile, I informed every larger boy in the school that there would be trouble for him if under Mrs Walter's tuition he 'played up', but it was unnecessary. The whole school was sobered by a hollow feeling of loss, of a presence utterly gone, bright day dimmed. None knew then that for three whole years Mrs Walter would 'hold the fort', as all her supporters expressed it, losing vital strength in maintaining what had been so well founded.

Before a first posting, in a brief home leave, we saw A. C. Walter's spare form in incongruous uniform, on the most unlikely sailor ever to be seen - the coarse navy-blue, the bell-bottomed trousers, only recently unfolded, the gleaming toe-caps, impeccable collar, the rakish angle of the peakless cap, proclaiming 'HMS' - with stance ready-made for the service, energy constrained but available on the word.

'I intend to be AB only,' he said, 'to be with the chaps who actually do the job,' and able-seaman he remained, fully determined on it, until 1919, demobilisation and his return to school. His contribution to the ultimate victory of the allied nations was entirely in destroyers guarding convoys in continuously dangerous waters, when he suffered severely in winter operations in the North Atlantic sea-lanes, sharing horrors especially affecting such as he - the sinking of merchant ships around him, the desperations of their crews, the sickening ramming of an enemy U-boat by his own boat and that vessel's crashing bisection, in the English Channel and fog, by an American troop ship, his narrow escape in the impact and then from drowning as his surviving forepart was beached, when the long exposure put him and most of the survivors into hospital for long periods. We were not told any of this until all was over, but in the following years we saw the permanent after-effects; the old dynamism was continuous no more.

In the strange summer term of 1916 Mrs Walter, tense and wan, had taken on brief responsibility for the two half-lost pupil-teachers along with full-time control of the school and so also the teaching of the upper forms. Lona and I sat amongst her older pupils and took part in some of her lessons, particularly those called 'Nature' on the timetable. I recall to this day one which revealed in her an almost loving thoroughness in that she required us to lay out, draw and carefully colour in all the parts of a garden wallflower, having before us a great bowl of these remarkably scented flowers from her garden. We saw teaching quite different from Mr Walter's, calmly done, too, although her home arrangements were then being urgently revised.

John Gamble insisted on 'doing' her garden - 'I'll not hear any nay, missis,' he said; his young daughter Margaret took on the school-time care of small Edith; Mrs Esther Chapman added school-house chores to her commitments in the school. 'Claydon folk rally round,' she said.

And I began my Saturday morning calls, determined to keep faith with her own words - 'Arthur said it is exactly what you would do.' Within only a day or two Lona and I received two identical letters from him from a far distant depot, including: 'Mr and Mrs Read - good people, you will soon discover.'

Pupil Teaching At Steeple Claydon School During The Great War 1916–19

I am again in the year 1916, the third troubled year of the First World War. First, A. C. Walter was away answering the Navy's call and Mrs Walter was finding her way as head of the school he had left in her care. Lona and I were little more than six months into our four-year bursaries. Mr Walter had been able to give us only the briefest introduction to our calling as very young pupil-teachers. Now we must contemplate continuation in the care of John Thomas Read, headmaster of Steeple Claydon School and he, his school and the village were all unknown to us.

By chance I had been accorded a view of him as he rode on his motorised cycle through our village one afternoon on a visit to Mr and Mrs Walter. He had persisted with this unique form of transport seen by some of our people once or twice before. He sat confidently high on his bicycle with the small motor popping merrily on the back wheel, relieving him, except at the rise into the village, of the need for the usual pedalling. He was a tall figure, slim and fully accoutred for the ride in overalls, reversed cap and goggles. Someone lower down in the village had given him a cheer. I at once aligned him in my mind with J. A. White as a progressive in the new age of the petrol-engine. Lona had acquired knowledge of him from her father who was abreast of all local matters and some farther off. He said: 'Read is more than a schoolmaster. For one thing he is a District Councillor - stands his ground and ruffles a few feathers too, mostly on Poor Law matters. He's on the Board of Guardians. People who know him well say he is something of a character.'

It was urgently necessary now that we acquire bicycles ourselves, for his school lay a good three miles distant. My father's small tease about Shank's Pony, and the shortest walk being through Claydon Park itself, was no more than that for he soon bargained for a bicycle for me. A village man had been 'directed by Government' to work up-the-line, that is, in the locomotive sheds of the Metropolitan Railway at Neasden, near London, to work on 'rolling-stock maintenance'. His second-hand model could pass third-hand to me for one pound which would pay his first week's lodging money in Neasden. Holding the heavy, elderly machine I judged the arrangement to be helpful all round as a war-time measure.

Lona secured a quite smart ladies' machine, complete with dress-guard, chain-guard and the fashionable small basked attached to the front of the handlebars. She proposed that we master our machines separately, wisely saying: 'To avoid riding into each other.' I was all for that, since with my saddle fully lowered mine was still a man's machine difficult to mount, heavy and strong-willed. It had been arranged that we would attach to Mr Read's school on the first day of June. As that day drew near I could ride in a fashion only, while Lona was not quite what she claimed to be when on the saddle. We could ride, but needed what my father, as an observer, called, 'plenty of side-room'. That we both lived beside the Weir Pond wonderfully concentrated out minds and our steering. Meanwhile, we received brief encouraging letters from A. C. Walter, headed only 'Haslar R. N. - May, 1916', saying: 'Mr John Thomas and Mrs Read - good people. Honour and pride of East Claydon School in your capable hands. Say not the struggle naught availeth - etc., etc.'

Then, as needs must, we set forth together in the bright sunlight of the first morning of the month which some say crowns the year. At fourteen years of age, both of us, it was our first venture in a new direction, so truly rural were our village communities then. Ours lay along the rounded top of a long, low hill and was familiar to us to the last brick, thatch, tree, garden, fence, field and inhabitant. For a while our way was known, but before long by way of winding roads, strange turnings, testing slopes, we reached the crossing of the Oxford-Cambridge railway and, immediately after that, must dismount at the foot of the steep hill we must climb, pushing our machines, to take our first view of Steeple Claydon, beginning with a near view of St. Michael's Church, whose spire we had seen often from afar. Mounted again, we came upon a wide spread of buildings, cottages, houses of the superior sort screened well by trees, a police station, a public house calling itself 'The Phoenix' and then the new-looking public hall and library. There we applied our brakes, because here suddenly the road fell away for a steep descent into a further wide spread of the village to bring into view, at its foot, the

Steeple Claydon School as it was until its recent demolition.
Photograph: Courtesy Mr George Rawlings

school, the bell tower and clock clearly identifying it.

With a little daring we descended through groups of chattering children, making for the open gateway into the school playground, entering a little too fast, our arrival reasonably well achieved until the last moment when my machine asserted itself in coming to a stop and rid itself of me, while Lona trippingly alighted, giving me a look of quiet scorn. She had seen what I, in my fierce concentration had not, two waiting figures, one very tall – Mr John Thomas and Mrs Read at his side.

Swiftly he stepped to me, raising my bicycle. 'Is all well?' he asked, while children ran to gather my scattered books, midday sandwiches and other belongings, giving them first into Mrs Read's care. Assured that all was well, they led us, smiling, into their school. We were in a rare mixture of first impressions, Lona calm, myself still a little ruffled. Children followed whispering: 'Who are they?' – 'Where are they from?' – 'Do you know them?' – 'Come to join the school, have they?'

Our 'Number Three Headmaster' (as privately we had named him) was very tall, hatless and of scanty hair, with eyes a gentle brown beneath sprouting eyebrows; above his readily smiling mouth was a short bristling moustache. His grey tweeds were of good quality but rumpled. Mrs Read was of erect, trim build, with an air of quiet precision about her. Her hair, greying and pleasingly waved, must have formerly been prettily fair. Her clear grey eyes broke into quick smiles. Her dress was a neat, purposeful, school overall.

'This way - this way,' they said together.

I saw that their school, although larger and newer, had been conceived on the same pattern as the 'Old School' of our beginnings. It was spotlessly clean and welcoming with bright pictures and charts on the walls, but its windows were all out of reach. We could not help comparing what we saw with the model school we had left, with its Henry Holiday's climbing children, its low clear-glass windows, the wall blackboards for children's use and the building's unusual and pleasing architecture. We had still to learn the truth of the truism that children and teachers make a school and to discover that the Reads knew how to do it. Morning school was being announced from the bell tower so we were led to the cloakroom arrangements and then to two desks placed at the back of the main form-room, Mr Read's own domain, where, rising at a third desk, Walter Thorpe, an earnest young man, explained that he was 'staying-on'.

'And now, what's best?' our new headmaster ventured. 'I'd say just spend time taking us all in today, though perhaps, for me, before the day is out, your "First Impressions" on this loose paper. I would be very happy if you will - just your own direct thoughts. I must leave you now.' I looked at my blank paper - it would be my first viewing of Steeple Claydon village, nothing further. As Lona was smiling I guessed she was thinking of our recent physical arrival. Sitting next to me, Walter Thorpe then said: 'Working for GPO exams - I take them when I'm sixteen,' and I to him: 'Prelim. Certif. for us when we're eighteen' - but more of Walter later, because he quickly became a pleasant, helpful companion. Through the day we toyed with our books, studied the unfamiliar changing scene and saw that, as at East Claydon, the head-teacher taught all the upper forms. We saw also that the wooden screen at our backs separated him and us from Mrs Read and her middle-school charges, her classroom door being next to us. In the lunch hour Walter Thorpe gave us a thorough viewing of the whole school and its precincts and in the afternoon Lona and I settled to our writing - in quantity not to let A. C. Walter down, but I doubted my quality because of the many unfamiliarities around us. It was no ordinary situation for two fourteen-year-old strangers designated pupil-teachers, very much more pupil than teacher. We were intensely grateful for our kindly reception and decided, as we pedalled homewards in the late afternoon, that the Reads would prove to be very interesting people.

Next day we sat to our course work, for Miss Rowlands, distant supervisor of pupil teachers, had apprised J. T. Read fully of all required of us and of him as our mentor and guide. 'Best to begin without delay,' he said, holding sheaves of paper; so we settled alongside Walter, fascinated to see that he knew exactly where he was heading. His was the first friendliness to come from our own kind. If most of Mr Read's pupils sitting near eyed us only curiously, several openly regarded us with suspicion. 'Take no notice of them,' Walter whispered, 'they will calm down. Yes,' he went on, 'staying on for the CPO exam - pretty stiff, they say. Mr Read helps me a lot.' It appeared that Walter was a career man in embryo, saturating himself in political geography and mathematics, with a facility in long-tots which boded well already. My Pendlebury's Arithmetic, proffered as a loan, made a swift opening to companionship in mental exercise and led to quick friendship between the three of us. His father was the steady postman whose red bicycle travelled the Claydon villages apparently from time immemorial; hence, perhaps, Walter's intention to go further, which, eventually he did, even as far as Mount Pleasant itself in London.

He delighted in challenges. With blank paper and pencil before him, and closed Atlas before me, I would say: 'Greece' - or 'Ireland' - or 'North Island of New Zealand', when swiftly from memory, he would trace an accurate outline, entering also the main mailing points, ports, sea-lines, railways, rivers, required for the direct transmission of mail thereto. Mentally I saw a great criss-crossing of the whole earth by sea and land, the sea-lanes reminding me of the miniature tracings made by the restless pond-skaters on the surface of the Weir Pond at home on a summer's day. As to his mathematics 'long-tots' were his speciality, the totalling of great columns of figures in brief time, while Pendlebury provided challenges of another sort, when I might select for him: 'Change 15,000 square yards into acres, roods, etc.,' on which he would say at once: 'Trying to catch me are you? Thirty-and-a-quarter square yards one square rod, pole or perch doesn't catch me' - nor did it. Lona tended to eschew all this, declaring it dull, while saying she supposed it was clever, our labours fortunately being on different lines.

From our desks, with a full view of J. T. Read's wide form-room and the near view of his main charges, we saw that in action he was a different manner of man from either A. J. White, or A. C. Walter, our sailor-man. After a spell of lively, often very interesting, class teaching he would put the class to close individual work sitting himself at his desk apparently lost in thought or, perhaps, dreams. We were amused to note that this was almost invariably helped by placing a fore-finger beneath his bristly moustache, a posture often silently and accurately copied by one lively class member when out of his view. 'Jim Henley,' Walter whispered. At one such moment, early on, Lona and I were afforded insight into interesting inter-play between 'JTR' and his wife, when, her classroom door placed wide open behind her, she quickly made a path to him, her sharp eye and frown setting James Henley smartly to his work again, as she tapped JTR's desk lid, bringing him to immediate awareness, saying: 'Have you? - you said you would. Don't say I must remind you' and he now: 'No - no, not yet, but, of course, now - now, dear, and without delay. But have you thought, Kit, on what I put to you?'

'Thought, of course, I've thought,' she replied, 'but first things first, hm?' - on which he rose to action saying: 'Of course, of course - course, course,' bending low to straighten an errant sock, then departing swiftly, murmuring to himself as he went, while she kept a splendid poise, assuming with it a gentle smile. Turning to return to her room she gave a light tap on the crown of James Henley's flaxen head. Something like this often occurred, always from something promised, postponed, forgotten, or lost in dream. Never, it seemed, could it happen in reverse. Walter had whispered: 'You'll see more of this.'

It could be even more interesting should it coincide with a change of lesson. She, having arrived for a session of music with his classes, would advance to the piano, seating herself very firmly, the children watchful and a little at loss, as she would say: 'How apt, dears. We did decide to being with "*Sigh no more, Ladies*" didn't we?' At which the introduction would be played precisely with a smile and no suggestion of the slightest sigh, by which time JTR would have retreated to her room for the change of lesson. In my young simplicity I soon sensed that they were very close - 'opposite poles', I thought.

Lona and I had a very close view of him each day in our hour after school, spent at his desk-side in the schoolroom. He had an exact timetable for this and our syllabus of work. Even here he might occasionally fall into dream, explained, we thought, by matters arising from the long hours of Council business of the previous evening? But he would arouse and say alertly: 'Now, where were we? Yes - Oliver Cromwell, Lord Protector, and don't forget the Verneys of Claydon House here - Edmund on the king's side, killed in the first battle of the Civil War, at Edgehill, not far from here, of course, and the red hand to this day on their escutcheon - and his brother Ralph, Parliamentarian, and so on the opposite side, writing those famous 'Notes on the Long Parliament'. And then the Royalist Dentons of Hillesdon, quite near us too, attacked by the Roundheads and yet Claydon House was not - because of Ralph, do you think? Anyway, take another look at the Camp Barn as you ride home. Oh - the Claydons were in the thick of it for a while.'

He had accepted our written 'First Impressions' with a smile, saying Lona had made our arrival quite vivid, while I, by concentrating on the village only, appeared to be opting for the diplomatic rather than the teaching service. 'Yes, indeed and thank you both,' he said, 'Mrs Read enjoyed your observations, too. And, by the way - a message from our lady supervisor. On the Saturday after next all her North Bucks pupil teachers are invited to take the annual tests at her Wolverton Grammar School - so that will be an experience, eh?' It would indeed, for we had first to discover how to get there, while feeling fearfully unprepared for it.

When the day came it passed in such a mixture of experiences that they are for me unclear to this day. First came the early morning cycle ride to Verney Junction Station to catch the cross-country train to take us to Bletchley, where main-line expresses roared through as we sought for the lesser train to bring us to Wolverton and the grammar school. All this was undertaken against time, for we were to be seated, pens poised, by ten-thirty sharp. There was one's desk in a spread of fifteen or so other sitters in a wide hall, our first view of Miss Rowlands herself and then, bustling in, Mr Boyce, the headmaster, to welcome us with words over-jolly as I thought. However, he left us to Miss Rowlands, in charge throughout the day. I saw her as quite young and business-like in her swishing gown and heard her as bright and brisk of speech. I recall sitting bemused before more than one examination paper in a day unreal all through and felt genuine relief to be leaving when dusk fell and Mr Boyce and Miss Rowlands shook hands with us all round. I decided that he must have considered us strange creatures – 'Ships that pass in the night', I thought unhappily. I knew I had not done well and Lona declared firmly that if we could have had A. C. Walter's help all through the year 'it would have been a different story'. J. T. Read said the same when we put our apprehensions to him on Monday morning. 'Put it all behind you,' he said kindly. 'I will see you right – never fear.'

But the putting behind us could not be done until we had shared another experience. Surely there was some desperation in the strange arrangement whereby we must cycle to Verney Junction Station again, to sit with Miss Rowlands in the waiting room for a post-mortem on our work, which appeared marked by much red ink and sometimes with exclamation marks – all this as freight trucks clanged and shunted, as the 'fast' thundered through within yards of us, to say nothing of Billy Janes', the porter's, brief intrusion, when, withdrawing, he said: 'Oh – I see—' which he did not – 'sorry, mum. Beg pardon.'

My enormity was the mishandling of a précis, completely overlaid in red; Lona's that she had ignored it altogether. In all its special nearness and strangeness the hour passed, Miss Rowlands saying that we mustn't be downhearted, must we, and that she must be alert for the Aylesbury train for a similar foray in another direction, so we envisaged her sitting in widely scattered waiting-rooms until dusk. On this JTR said: 'We shall hear from the dear lady quite soon, then. Strange that the word 'précis' bemused you. We must put that right if it isn't remedied already, hm? We live and learn, don't we?' and then to himself: 'Or we're nothing.' He set about putting us right and our visits to Wolverton for testings in 1917 and 1918 entailed no further emergency meetings in railway stations while enabling us to know a little more of our fellow pupil teachers.

Inevitably from the moment of our arrival at their school some of the older pupils had regarded us with suspicion as specially favoured incomers little older than themselves, although Lona had a relatively easy passage under the wing of tall, slim and kindly Miss Weston of the infant classes. She herself when young, had been a pupil-teacher. She tactfully enrolled Lona as 'helper' of the small beginners when at their play and games and some of their first teaching.

Mr Read wisely asked nothing of me with regard to leadership as A. C. Walter had, for I had yet to be accepted by his older boys. I think he knew that a testing time would come and that I must deal with it myself. Meanwhile, I must bear with a whispered: 'Who does he think he is?' and a sudden heavy bump in the privacy of the cloakroom, followed by: 'Sorry - sorry, *sir*. Didn't see you.'

Walter stood by me when the inevitable happened, when Joe West cornered me to explain, so that all gathering to us could hear, that I was nothing like a teacher, nor ever would be, that I need not throw my weight about in Steeple Claydon, coming as I did from a place of no account at all and so, what about it? Eyes narrowed, fists whitened and I must, perforce, make a stand to cries of: 'That's it, Joe - stand up to him. Do they know how to fight where he comes from? - bet he's a cowardy-custard.' Walter murmured: 'You'll have to settle with him,' and we all repaired to the rear of the school, J. T. and Mrs Read and staff being well away at lunch.

We shaped up and Walter withdrew having whispered valuable information of Joe's vulnerable points and parts. It must result in a suitable end, though Joe was of tough, bony build, and I must avoid dishevelment, so it became a grim sort of wrestling match with much puffing and blowing, gritting of teeth, swaying and grunting until I achieved the hold I wanted, the Japanese grip I had studied in a fascinating manual in the village reading-room at home. On Walter's pre-match advice I declared the result 'evens', Joe having gruntingly to agree. On this, I was taken to be a reasonable being after all, and the atmosphere changed almost at once. Having known boys in their hundreds since that fateful day, I would not now be as surprised at this as I was then.

In the afternoon, as Walter and I ambled amongst the boys in their playground during 'break', JTR appeared and joined us.

'Settling in, I see,' he said, 'Capital - capital.' Had he known about the lunch time episode? If so he gave no hint of it and went on: 'I foresee for you both in your different ways,' but he did not say what he foresaw and soon left us. As we watched him go Walter said: 'I reckon he knew and I reckon he knew it would be Joe West.'

Lona and I were by this time comprehending JTR's whole organisation, an establishment larger than that we had left, for the village population was probably double. So there were the large schoolroom where he operated; the middle room for middle forms, with Mrs Read as his sheet-anchor there; two infant rooms with Miss Weston in charge and a further room for first and second year pupils in the care of a Miss Payne, not now clear in my memory except for a moment when, quite unaware, she threw for us an amusing light on JTR himself. She had prowess on the piano and regularly performed on it in the lunch hour when JTR's room was empty and echoing. Lona and I often came to listen to her flamboyancy, for that is what it was, her support a volume entitled 'Happy Hours on the Pianoforte'. On this occasion she arrived with it already open, smiling and saying: '*The Robin's Return* - know it?', opening up at once with the lightest of tinklings which took her the full length of the keyboard and back again. At this moment the room door opened and JTR strode to his desk, raising the lid for something needed, pausing, astonished, to gaze at the pianist and then at us with a look of genuine consternation, or, shall we say, of concerned wonder? Miss Payne had not seen him and, caught up now with her resounding interpretation, proceeded to bring out not only her returned robin but a whole nestful of his companions in such a state of delirium that she shook the piano down to its pedals. JTR, desk lid in hand, turned pale, then dropped the lid, turned and fled from the room exclaiming: 'Oh - no! Dear, dear, oh dear!' We sat in wonderment, but Miss Payne swayed and played on to the end all unknowing, turning at the end to say: 'Shall I play it again?' Lona, enthralled, said: 'Yes, please, Miss Payne,' while I sat in astonishment considering the failure of JTR's mission to his desk and how at the very moment he might be explaining it to Mrs Read and perhaps, also the danger to the piano of which she always had first use. However, neither of them appeared and I crept away for the second rendition, retreating to the Infants' Room and Miss Weston's piano, there to toy a little - the door closed - with one of Mendelssohn's simpler *Songs Without Words*.

JTR appeared to have recovered by afternoon school. He gave us a distant quizzical smile, with a nod in the direction of the piano, as he began his teaching. This was so regularly enlivened by the unexpected, by oral, pictorial, or any other handy illustration, that it was always worthwhile to keep an eye on him as we ourselves worked. And, as I have said, in the room behind us was Mrs Read, born to be a teacher and available to provide example and interest at any moment. She possessed the warming smile and, when required the warning one and the all-seeing eye. It was fascinating to hear her quiet voice saying: 'This work will not do. It must be done again - better. Look - I will begin it for you. Bring me what you have done five minutes from now; and the time now is . . .? Off you go and look cheerful.' She had taken to teaching as ducklings to water - eagerly with no trouble at all and with a high intelligence, while he, with an intelligence equally high, must have dropped absent-mindedly into it, deciding that he must sink or swim and then that swim he would and so made quite a unique thing of it. It was plain to us that he had come to firm conclusions on what education for young people should be about.

We saw something of this when the Local Education Authority, sitting solemnly in Aylesbury, devised and imposed standard tests in Basic English and Arithmetic upon the upper forms in all the county schools designated elementary. He was deeply angered and said with asperity: 'Who needs strait-jackets? Who needs hounding into competency? Don't they know that what cannot be measured is by far the most important? But we are not afraid of them, are we - about the hum-drum stuff?' He was not perturbed when the great moment came with his own candidates busying away in the prescribed hour. He came over to his three observers to whisper: 'Treasure this great thought, this awesome moment, that hundreds of the sons and daughters of Bucks are now lighting upon a momentous discovery - that a certain number of ounces are equal to one ton of house coal - and, by the way, how do you envisage an ounce of coal?' He stood smiling down, particularly at Walter whose brow was wrinkled on the mental calculation before jotting down the swift result, when JTR whispered again: 'Yes, Walter - of course, mail goes by weight.' This must have occurred at, or near, Walter's sixteenth birthday for about now he left to pass his demanding examinations with ease, I am sure and to begin his climb in the mighty Postal Service. He had been a good stalwart companion and friend. For two years the Reads had aided him in his ambition.

The instant drive and verve of A. C. Walter were lacking in J. T. Read, nor did he have anything like the vigour of A. J. White. Certainly he never thought that a difficult boy should 'walk' for punishment. Resort to that he would regard as utter failure. His procedures on failings were amusing to watch but were effective. In the case of a boy he would exclaim: 'Ass - ass - dolt. Wretched creature - have you lost your senses?', and to a girl, apparently meaning it with considerable vehemence and looking thoroughly aggrieved, he would say: Alas - alas! Oh, dear me - to what depths are we falling, if not sinking from sight? You must really give thought to your actions, you definitely must.' The erring ones would subside and recoil, sometimes go pale and mend their ways lest a thunder-bolt fall.

In our tutorial hours with him Lona and I discovered that he was able enough, with our hum-drum stuff, but that literary, historical, artistic and sociological matters were his forte. He might fall into a temporary dream over our physical geography, or a batch of teasing vulgar fractions but never over, say, *Piers Plowman* and his 'fair field full of folk', or our local John Hampden and the ship-money, or the Great Reform Act of 1832, or taking on our next Shakespeare play well ahead of Miss Rowland's timetable, or putting us to Thomas Hardy - perhaps a trifle too soon.

It was significant too, and regarded locally as a wonder, that he had obtained a Bachelor of Arts degree from Trinity College, Dublin, while continuing his headship of the school. Long hours of study and long miles of travel demanded his complete dedication and Mrs Read's full help and support. Results were to be seen in the school-house - piles of books, current periodicals, cultural, political, social, and also by what he brought into school, often in an excitement bound to be caught by some of the young hopefuls before him. For example: 'Here is something I bought in Oxford last Saturday, a fine book as you can see. Pass it quietly round as you work. Tell me later what you think of the pictures - handle it carefully.' The something could have been illustrated remarkably by Arthur Rackham. He acted as proof-reader for Lady Margaret Verney, of Claydon House, whose *Bucks Biographies* told of the county's worthies of the past - inevitably Cromwell's own cousin, John Hampden whose statue stands in Aylesbury's main square, and John Milton, who moved to Chalfont St. Giles when the Great Plague broke out in London, to continue his writing though blind, proving that 'God's talent which is death to hide' was not lodged with him useless. Then there was the gentle, humane William Cowper of Olney, who immortalised Mary Unwin equally with himself in his writings and Thomas Gray, who made the country churchyard at Stoke Poges known forever and many another, not forgetting Lady Margaret's own renowned aunt, Florence Nightingale, living out her old age at Claydon House. It is good to read there Florence's own words supporting the establishment of the three Claydon village libraries: 'Success will be slow, but what ripens too fast, what is forced, is not what lasts the longest.' So she helped with money for books for the first village free libraries in the land. In my youth I had much use of them.

Connection with the 'House' brought the advantage of school visits. I recall joining the crocodile of children and teachers for the long walk though and from the village, then downhill and across the park to reach the impressive home of the Verney family, settled there

Claydon House at Middle Claydon – 'the home of Miss Florence Nightingale'. A postcard of 1908. Florence Nightingale had a house of her own in London, but, especially in her later years, she often stayed with her sister, Parthenope Verney, at Claydon House where she had rooms of her own.
Postcard: Hubert Chapman

over three centuries. We had to see the portrait of King Charles the First by Van Dyck, the astonishing Chinese Room, the clever, graceful stucco high on the walls, the work of craftsmen from France and Italy, the strangely formed main staircase with its delicate balustrade of fine iron-work - growing corn, which actually rustled as one mounted the inlaid treads, wearing the felt slippers provided. But most particularly I am in the Grand Saloon with a whole school party seated on the largest and most comfortably yielding carpet we had ever seen, listening to young Sir Harry Verney playing on the organ curious Chinese music contrasting with the lively western music we all knew, with gentle Lady Rachel Verney sitting beside us, happy to see us so absorbed.

We were led in this way to an interest in the Verney family and their place in English history, especially in the troubled times of the Civil War. This led me, later, to the illuminating *Verney Memoirs*, put together from the family papers discovered by the late Lady

Parthenope Verney, Florence Nightingale's sister, in a long neglected storehouse in the great courtyrard. She had had the help of Lady Margaret in placing before the public this piece of first-hand social history, now widely known. As a budding teacher, browsing among these in the village library, I was struck by the letter-writing of the lady correspondents of the seventeenth and eighteenth centuries, who, though readily articulate, spelt as they pleased and often with a very direct homeliness. The Memoirs show what a centre of activity Claydon House then was. 'The House' and the locality were inter-dependent over generations, as, of course, they still were in considerable measure in JTR's day.

'Yes,' said John Thomas Read, 'One Edmund slain at Edgehill in 1642, holding the royal standard, another Edmund only recently laid to rest at Middle Claydon and now his son, young Sir Harry, Liberal Member of Parliament for North Bucks - we're bound to be interested! Another expedition took us by field paths to the nearby village of Hillesdon where the Roundhead troops had besieged the home of the Denton family. We had to see the oak door still bearing the marks of musket-balls. It began in me the small shiver I felt whenever I contemplated the painting entitled: *And when did you last see your father?* For a moment, I was a straight-backed young Denton.

An expedition to Oxford followed. One Saturday the Reads took Lona and me and a small band of older pupils for 'a day immersed in history', as JTR expressed it when we boarded our train at Claydon LNWR Station, saying also as we settled: 'An essay from each one of you in return, please - title agreed *Oxford Moments*, or something like that?' The city's dreaming spires lay twenty miles distant from the high point in our Claydon Woods and I may have claimed, in a boy's boasting, that I had seen them gleam on a clear day; but that day we moved amongst them, craned upward to view them, wondered at the ancient stonemasons' ingenuity and varieties, tried to imagine their building by clever men long passed away - so many churches requiring spires, so many great colleges boasting towers! We headed first for the Ashmolean Museum where Lord Leighton's *Flaming June* brought me at once to a stand, drew me to it as by a magnet, to see what a great artist can do with a mass of colour to astound eye and mind. And who painted the wood pigeons sitting close on house eaves in bright sunshine, but with gleaming rain drops on them from a storm just passed? I have forgotten, but the picture - Pre-Raphaelite? - is with me any time I close my eyes - the silky reality of the birds' plumage, the wetness of the glinting rain drops. JTR smiled down on me, without a word, as I stood before them amazed. We moved on to University College to look down in awe upon the poet Shelley prostrate in white marble, to feel something of the loss laid out on the shore at Spezzia in Italy on that fateful day in July, 1822. As I stood there I knew that this would be my written 'moment'. However beautifully done the cold marble spoke terribly of a spirit lost, quenched and gone forever - a rarest of spirits which society could ill afford so tragically to lose. Truly he himself had written: *When the cloud is scattered the rainbow's glory is shed.*

The immaculate lawns and gardens of St. John's College, where we went for quiet contemplation and rest, were needed after that, but soon we must make our way to Blackwell's Bookshop, Mrs Read smiling broadly as JTR led the way. On arrival he said: 'Fine books, Kit - I must look at the new remainders.'

'You will and thoroughly,' she said, 'and I must go to the Education side - for *contes* of a simple sort for Joan and these young people.' In preparation for Wycombe Abbey School their daughter of ten or eleven years was requiring 'some French' and her mother was giving Lona and me the benefit of joining them.

But I had to find Chaundy's, to make haste to their second-hand bookcases and shelves, where my painfully limited money was turned over in a bewilderment of books. Overseen by our distant Miss Rowlands, Lona and I, with JTR, were 'doing' the fourteenth century before the Black Death, the period which so enchanted William Morris, so that he had put a kind of glow on it as a halcyon time lost. And yes, Chaundy's had a used copy of *A Dream of John Ball* and so 'When Adam delved and Eve span, who was then the gentleman?' it had to be. My cash now spent put out of consideration *The Gathering of Brother Hilarius*, the recent lightweight by Michael Fairless. It took in the Black Death period itself, but I could not afford both and so hurried back to Blackwells.

There our party was widely spread among the shelves and JTR already had a find firmly clutched and was saying: 'And you? Oh yes, John Ball - well done. First rate introduction to books this for our young people, don't you think? - eyes and minds opening together. By the way, while on all this, discover who wrote '*A good book is the precious life-blood of a master spirit*' and tell me on Monday how it continues. Vilona is searching even now.' He liked devising small missions of this kind. Christ Church, the Martyrs' Memorial, Cardinal

Wolsey's huge kitchens, Magdalen Tower - did we add them that day? I forget, for I well recall our cycle ride home at the end of that long day. By the time we arrived, Oxford still with us, my piece on the Shelley Memorial was more than half compiled. What Lona wrote I do not know, but in my young conceit I registered JTR's words on reading mine in the Monday hour: 'Yes - thought it would be Shelley for you - yes, indeed, the deadness of the cold marble - yes.'

He was deeply impressed by the young writers drawn into the war and brought to our tutorial hour the poems of Wilfred Owen, Robert Nichol, Siegfried Sassoon, Isaac Rosenberg, the ink scarcely dry on the pages - could it have been, of The Clarion?

'Purged and moulded in the fires,' he said, 'they speak for all young folk while they can,' but he did not dwell on the war with the children. 'The war poets are not for them yet,' he said; 'First, they are for the leaders of nations and so, also, for us.' I found J. C. Squire's *To a Bull-dog* for myself and fought and shed unashamed tears over it.

As had A. C. Walter, he fretted that our syllabus of work was too narrow. 'Thorough in a small field,' he said, 'but we need to expand on it - the cultural side is so important.' Thus, wider and wider reading was pressed upon us. 'Heavens!' he said, 'you have three

East Claydon Village Hall, Library and Clocktower today.
Photograph: Gillian Spencer

village libraries to draw upon. Find out what life was like when your great-grand-parents were your age. See also how great artists help us on this in ages farther back - the Dutch painters on ordinary folk, our own Gainsborough on those who commissioned him' and on these he would bring in examples, reproductions of his own.

'What are you reading now - anything, say, of George Meredith?' he would ask and when I replied, *The Ordeal of Richard Feverel*, he cried: 'Good gracious me! I think it ought to be *Harry Richmond* if you want to go on with that man. And Lona, what about you?' She said that 'Gentle Jane' Austen was enough. 'Just as well,' he said, 'but not so gentle she, as you will soon find out.' However, I met frustration in our East Claydon library. It was well stocked with reference books and well-established fiction, many books given by benefactors from their own shelves. There was much there to absorb me. The fiction side was regularly used and readers came to exchange books in a pleasant hour each Friday afternoon. It was the suggestion book, seeking ideas for additional reading, which troubled me. My requests for Thomas Hardy's *Tess of the D'Urbervilles*, and, failing that, *Jude the Obscure* brought no result, yet after a month or so of apparently careful consideration, *A Pair of Blue Eyes* was allowed and appeared, meeting at last my daring request on behalf of the country's great novelist of the day. Others' hopes for the works of Elinor Glyn, Ruby M. Ayres, Dorothy Conyers, Ethel M. Dell and, of course, Marie Corelli, were at the same time quickly and plentifully met.

I mentioned this to JTR, who, smiling a little, bent to raise and straighten a silk sock, which regularly aided thought. Rising, he said: 'Ah - I'm not surprised, but don't disparage the lady writers you speak of: they start the village wives reading whole books. It's a different matter with Hardy, though. Village library committees go carefully on him. I know some of the members over there. Chapel and church are both on the watch for dangerous print. It would have been better to being with *A Pair of Blue Eyes*, though there is there the rescue by the torn petticoat' and here he laughed aloud. 'Mind you, they may not have read it through - and certainly not "Tess" or "Jude", well able to pronounce and decide on them, and on you, for that matter, without that.'

'As to Tess Darbyfield's family and the D'Urbervilles' - and here, for a moment, he fell a little into dream, 'Have you given any thought to our own Duckmanton family? You've helped small Amy with her reading, Vilona.' I had puzzled often over the unusual name attached to smiling Amy. 'Duc,' JTR then carefully said, 'don't you see? French, without doubt and now put "Manton" behind it and pronounce all as I do - Duc D'Manton. What about that? You've seen the fine plaster work, the stucco, in Claydon House. Foreign craftsmen were employed on that special work in the great houses in the past. Some stayed and married local women and their descendents became much the same as their neighbours in a generation or two.' Quiet observation of Amy's plump form and cheerful physiognomy, her eyes brown - not the local blue, grey, or hazel - seemed to confirm JTR's thought. I wondered whether Amy's family wondered about it as the schoolmaster, and now we two, wondered. Considerations of this sort often led him to put aside Miss Rowland's requirements of us, which then necessitated setting extra homework, especially for the weekends. He dwelt often on matters of the day and saw to it that we too thought about them. He inveighed against the nationalisms which had brought about the war; he deplored the inadequacies of an education system which sent the majority of the nation's children into the world of work at the moment when they had acquired only the basic tools of learning and only the beginning of an understanding of the riches of art and literature; he declared the system of tied-cottages for men who worked on the land to be wrong and the meagreness of their weekly wage to be a national shame - 'Why half-starve those who now are saving the nation from starving?' Active on the local Board of Guardians, as Lona's father had reported, he spoke of his official visits to the Winslow poor-house, the last home of many after a lifetime of labour, where husbands and wives were firmly accommodated apart at the last. On this he murmured: 'Cold as charity ten days cold' - something a bitter old man had quoted to him. He spoke of an Endowment of Motherhood years before anything like it was instituted and so was designated a Socialist in some quarters, although he was simply an active, thinking Liberal in a Liberal countryside. Lona and I shared his pleasure in admiring the tramping man, who made the Winslow poor-house his home in the winter months, doing his tally of wood-sawing, splitting and chopping for his keep, but who would stay not a moment longer when spring stirred - 'I've seen me first primmy-rose, you see, sir,' he had confided to JTR. We felt certain that JTR had quietly given him 'a little help' to start him on the road again.

His forays in book and art shops brought him his collection *One Hundred Great Paintings*, good quality, fairly large-scale reproductions of the work of artists through the centuries, in folders, five or six in each. The Dutch and other works shown to Lona and me came from these. On Friday afternoons, week after week, in the final period of the school week, he carried into school two folders and the current book for his oral reading, when the children sat expectant and Lona, Walter and I suspended our work. So, with R. L. Stevenson's, *Treasure Island* brightly book-marked in his hand and the folders laid before him on his desk, he would say: 'Which first today – Jim or the paintings?' to win the response: 'Please, sir – pictures first and finish with *Treasure Island*. Here, our own Tommy Hawkins would look round the class and give a shrug, his ever-wide smile growing wider, because he identified a little with his famous name-sake of the apple barrel and we all knew it. 'So be it,' John Thomas Read would say, taking up the upper folder, opening it wide and bringing it forward for all to see. 'We begin, as usual, with recognition,' he said. 'Take your time with this – take a long look. Dick Dalton has first chance today. Now, Dick, who drew this about four hundred years ago?' If Dick did not respond, despite nudgings and whisperings: 'Open to all, then – who's first?' would follow, when Phyllis Stephens would say, half questioningly: 'The German who done the rabbit?', for JTR to nod pleased and say: 'Correct – Albert Durer, but best to say *did* and not *done*, Phyllis, dear – good girl, though. Look, I will write his name on the blackboard, German, as you say, Phyllis, and' – turning a page – 'see, here is Phyllis's rabbit.' Then he would display another masterpiece and another, finishing 'recognition', with a smile and Hans Holbein's portrait of 'England's fat rascal', King Henry the Eighth. He would turn then to the second folder and to one painting only, one not displayed before, for a long look at it, a talk about it and the artist with an invitation to comment – all lightly done. From all this watching from the back, and being myself familiar with shire and other horses as working friends, by this time I could distinguish between George Morland and Rosa Bonheur when it came to a forge or stable scene; while Lona, asking again for a view, would sigh dreadfully over Ophelia floating in the stream ('by Millais, not Millet, for goodness sake') while Walter absentmindedly doodled map outlines on a scrap of paper, his eyes fixed on JTR, saying: 'I shall remember this.' Finally, we were told 'where this painting may be seen' and where 'that has hung as long as I can remember – but now to our book.' Then he would begin to read aloud looking pointedly over at Lona and me, his expression clearly saying: 'Take note'.

Never was there such a smooth-tongued and deadly Long John Silver, nor so many boys perspiring in the apple-barrel with Jim and Tommy Hawkins; nor ever so poignant an understanding of poor castaway Ben Gunn's fate and his desperate longing for a bite of English cheese. In the same way *Westward Ho!* took up a long run of Friday readings. Of this I remember with deep pleasure how the children turned to me with ready smiles, when he read how Sir Amyas Leigh, home again from the hazards of the Spanish Main, after long absence, has brought for his dear wife a beautiful silk scarf, saying: 'I had it from a chapman in the streets.' As the listeners turned back to JTR for more they did not know how far down the years I would take their smiles. 'Nothing of this is measurable,' he would say, 'nothing at all. The worthwhile things are ever better caught than taught.'

The effect of all this on me was to steer me in directions ready and waiting, more and more towards the literary, historical, artistic and sociological aspects of our course work, leaving the other required aspects, which JTR called the hum-drum, to become no more than adequate, although I did become keen on the one and only science, namely Botany, which sent me into the fields, hedgerows and woods for the living side of it all. Gradually, I developed a lasting imbalance of interests, although I also caught something of JTR's growing interest, even excitement, in the technical innovations that were already exciting the world. He was proud that he had stood amongst those invited to the Terrace of the House of Commons for Marconi's demonstration, over its length, of the transmission of his amazing signal. He was more proud still that his family was connected to one of the pioneers in the new exciting field of heavier-than-air aeronautics. On the basis of that the Reads' young son had been christened John Harris Farman Read after Farman who made the first bi-plane to rise - a little - from the earth. This young Read, at ten years of age, also evinced a desire to rise in the air and did this by climbing to the peak of the school roof one lunchtime, to sit astride the roof tiles waving to the gathering watchers below. Arriving among them, JTR, worried but proud, called: 'Ass of a boy! Stop waving and hold firmly to that chimney. Now you have done it, do you know how to come down?' But it was Mrs Read's calmness which brought him safely to earth: 'Do come down, John. You have shown you can do it.' We were all aware of what pioneer airmen like Farman had done and followed the increasing importance of flight in the war. Men were getting into flimsy machines for combat and observation in the battle-zones and Count Zeppelin in Germany had made the creeping monster, armed with bombs, which invaded our island's air space to be brought crashing to earth at Billericay, in Essex, Mrs Read's home-place. What is more, she possessed a souvenir from the wreckage - a scrap of twisted aluminium. Had this inspired her own young Farman to test Steeple Claydon's upper air? At least, it made a diversion the village thoroughly enjoyed. JTR's alert mind dwelt long on what the impetus of war was doing to the petrol engine, using it widely himself, as a matter-of-course, to extend his personal travel.

Such things weighed with him, but his commitment to us as embryo teachers was continuous and deeply considered. Class-teaching, into which we must be introduced more and more was always done under his, or Mrs Read's supervision, mainly as reliefs to them in dictation work; furbishments of arithmetical tables and rules; with bright mental work, oral reading and spelling-bees. As I grew older I took the boys' physical education and games entirely from him. Lona could have had no better guide than Mrs Read in the needlework classes. Darning, patching, knitting and the construction of new garments from old became urgent as the war's stresses increased. I supposed that, apart from the war's additional requirements and strains, entry into teaching ran generally on these lines.

Through these troubled years John Thomas Read provided stimulus to our thought and to our fast-growing social awareness, regularly laying an array of daily newspapers before us - 'essential to read all views,' he said. He deplored the futility of wars to settle anything and read to us the increasing body of poetry by young men caught up in the current battlefields. I met Wilfred Owen's *Strange Meeting* then and felt later the dreadful irony of his dying just as, in a sort of huge exhaustion, the great conflict was ending. I learned that Robert W. Service was right in his simple way with '*What's the use of a cross to 'im?*' - speaking for his homely fellow Canadians, on the Western Front in France, caught up in a horror of machine-gunfire, star shells and shell holes in a hellish muddy quagmire thousands of miles from home. It all ended in November, 1918 one month after my seventeenth birthday and in the third year of our bursaries. So the Armistice came and quite soon I felt with Siegfried Sassoon the slow lifting of spirits when the booming barrages fell away and then were silent, so that suddenly *Everyone Sang* and could sing to be heard once again.

But on the day of armistice our villages at first knew nothing. It was a day of steady, fine rain, semi-darkness, muddy roads and sodden fallen leaves. When at the day's end JTR asked me to ride home by way of Winslow Town with a missive for his friend the headmaster there, I thought of it as no more than something I would readily do, having cheerfully ridden for him many times. The morning papers had spoken of the Allies' great push at Capaume on the Western Front, showing the salient made at last in the Hindenberg Line, speaking also of the 'enemy withdrawing in disorder', so I suppose I thought of this as I rode the muddy lanes between the rain-sodden road-side fields, under bare trees dripping in showers, until the dimmed lighting of the town came into view. Soon I stood at Mr Pass's house door flung wide open, his lighting steaming out, while he was beaming upon me and saying: 'Don't you *know*? Armistice signed this morning. It's all over at last - telephones buzzing all day. In with you - off with those wet clothes. Celebrate with tea and hot toast.' So I celebrated with Mr George Pass and his wife and then sped home through the darkness, as fast as my wheels would turn, to be first with the news at The Weir, Botolph Claydon and so to be, on this great occasion, at least one step ahead of Miss Lona.

Within three months I would have been required to register for military service and after three further months of minimal training would have been liable to face the woebegone young conscripts of the other side. *Strange Meeting* would have been mightily strange and sobering then. I learned later that the Kaiser of those German boys, 'Big Willie' of our early scorn, had declined to visit his battle-worn troops the moment that 'field-grey' became imperative uniform throughout his armies, because the wearing of his magnificent field-marshal's uniform 'was not advised'. Could this had been known to us at the time the revelation would have electrified our headmaster to the heights of bitter comment: 'Such people lead us into horrors and then can neither extricate themselves, or us,' would have been the gist of it.

A full year before the Armistice, he had made another great historical moment thoroughly memorable, if not fully understood by us in his school. October 1917 saw him enter in a rush, bearing an armful of newspapers, crying: 'Close all books - put down your pens and listen,' telling us of a terrible, and inevitable revolution in Russia - great and terrible like the French Revolution had been. We must try to understand that as we sat there in our village school, far away from it all, a tremendous turning-point in history had come about, which would affect our lives for years to come. The whole world was being shaken and would never be the same again. We must try – try to understand what had happened and why. The great roll-map of Europe was brought out. Russia trembled under his pointer, Moscow and St. Petersburg, where it was all happening. The newspapers with their staring black headlines passed from hand to hand. How much was understood by his startled and puzzled young listeners is a matter for question: for his older watchers JTR created an occasion never to fade.

By the Armistice Lona and I had begun the final year of our bursaries and the red ink of our supervisor increased in intensity. I can see again the puckered brow of our zealous headmaster as he sighed over it and I hear again his murmured words: 'Perhaps – perhaps,' or to us: 'Good heavens – this on Malvolio! My Gervinus will suffice for us, surely.' He was a sound ally. We were amused that the scholar in him made the good lady's comments as great a concern to him as they were meant to be for us.

We now entered the year 1919, which saw the return to the Claydon villages of many of the surviving service men and with them came A. C. Walter from the navy, when he relieved Mrs Walter of the headship of his East Claydon school. Soon he and Mrs Walter began their help with my revision work for the approaching 'Prelim', by providing an upper room for my evening study, along with the ever-to-be-remembered reward of hot cocoa to conclude each session. So was I fortified for the two days of final tests in June in Miss Rowland's school at Wolverton. Unhappily, Lona had succumbed to the virulent influenza which was distressing the whole country at that time and so was compelled to postpone her tests. My experience of it had been light and consequently I travelled alone. The fifteen or so candidates gathered for the last time were, as in previous summers, either diffident or over cheerful as Miss Rowlands arrived to introduce us to the 'scene of execution', as one trite soul ventured to describe it – that is, to the school's main hall with single desks extravagantly placed well apart. As we stood, each to our own, Mr Boyce, her headmaster, entered to welcome us with attempts at jollity, saying: 'The final throw, then? Anyone here from Linslade, or Twyford, of Maids Moreton – No? Anyway, smiles all round, please. I wish for you all the right questions.' On this he left us. I sat again amongst fellow pupil teachers, fully knowing none of them, wondering about their capacities and doubting my own with every passing minute as I worked at the strangely printed question papers, while watching, in my thoughtful pauses, Miss Rowlands splendidly gowned and raised on high invigilating to the last splutter of our pen nibs.

In breaks for refreshment Mr Boyce came into the hall again, seeking to ease our tensions, but sometimes instead raising alarms about a paper irrevocably done, then stating that probably he was wrong and that we, 'being fresher to the work in hand', no doubt, knew better than he. Over coffee and sandwiches he was amusing on the harshness to the throat of the National Loaf and the weirdness of the cocoa-butter in the sandwiches, going on to introduce us to the latest wonder, the saccharine wafer, which you placed on the surface of your coffee, where it floated for a moment and then sank to provide a much too sweet, and peculiar sweetness. 'Out of the laboratories came forth sweetness - eh?' he joked. It was heavy going for him and for Miss Rowlands because our minds were always on the next session and also on what might have been better done an hour ago - or yesterday.

Two long days and all was over. He and Miss Rowlands shook hands with us all round, she saying that it had been such a pleasure getting to know us through our work and he that he was certain we had all passed with honours, though on what he based that optimism was totally unclear. On that we left to go our several ways home.

Examinations of this sort being what they are, this one provided me with a bewildering result - a Distinction in History and Passes only in all other subjects, including English Literature in which my hopes had ridden high and in Geography in which I was positive that I had failed. A. C. Walter and J. T. Read agreed that it was a 'minor travesty' and both that I would justify myself 'ere long.

The important thing was that I was now 'Uncertif', that is, 'Uncertificated but Recognised' by the great Board of Education in London and so deemed fit to go forth into the world as a full-time teacher to do what I could for young people of five to fourteen years of age and, furthermore, I was now qualified to proceed to training college for full certification and goodness only knew what grandeurs after that.

The First World War and East Claydon

When A C Walter had stood before us in May 1916, a smilingly incongruous able-seaman-to-be, assigned as yet to no vessel, the Great War was well into its second year. Its effects were then reaching far into all the Claydon villages. Although Lona and I were about to spend five days a week for more than three years in Steeple Claydon, getting to know the larger village and making lasting friendships there, inevitably the folk and affairs of our own village homes were paramount with us because of the war's demands, with its increasing privations and alarms as men known to us were taken by it, some never to return. We had not been pupil-teachers long when news came that Charlie Whitmarsh and his mine-sweeper, the 'Jackdaw', were forever lost somewhere in the North Sea, while young fellows only a few years older than I were being called up to war service.

A C Walter was briefly home again in October, on posting leave from the Royal Naval Camp, Haslar, Portsmouth. Every moment was precious to him and Mrs Walter and puzzled small Edith. He pressed Lona and me to write and write to him (for Mrs Walter was already too far engaged in school matters for much of that) with news of the village, of our progress towards 'Prelim' and our own experience of 'foreign parts', Steeple Claydon and its people. We promised and I kept my promise to the war's end and beyond. He was now a very smart able-seaman as he left to join the destroyer 'Rival' in a port he must not name. His last pointed words to me were: 'From you, young sir, I want the Claydon hedges, fields, trees, gardens, above all the scent of wild honeysuckle, if we get round to summer 1917. I depend on you. I will write in return.'

By this time Lona and I were firmly in the care of J. T. Read at Steeple Claydon, so not until Saturday morning could I head with paintbox and brushes to Mrs Walter's silent Big Room in the East Claydon school, there to make and illustrate the November weather calendar for Miss Wyatt and her infants. A 'different surprise for the infants became a regular commitment month by month until A. C. Walter himself should return to continue what he had begun for them in January. I could do little more than this directly to help Mrs Walter in school, apart from keeping a friendly eye on her largest boys who, in rough and ready ways, appeared to like her. I possess still my watercolour sketch of the lark rising before Miss Wyatt and her charges in June, 1916.

I noticed now that Miss Gwendolyn Verney of Botolph House in the village was calling often at the East Claydon schoolhouse. No one could be more unobtrusively kind and helpful. Many in the village knew of the help she and her long-widowed mother quietly gave when families fell into difficulties because of illness, accident, or sudden tragic blows from the war. Both had immediately liked A. C. Walter and at once encouraged and helped Lona and me in our beginnings as pupil teachers.

Our visit to the St. James's Theatre in London was under their auspices, while Miss Gwendolyn herself saw to it that our former headmaster's hope that we should visit Stratford-upon-Avon should be realised. One memorable Saturday she took us by railroads now no longer existing to a day of wonder when we sat in the old Memorial Theatre of Shakespeare unforgettably live again – 'As You Like It', with, perhaps (for now I forget) the young and beautiful Peggy Ashcroft as Rosalind?

Printed also in my young memory from that long summer day are Colonel Tom Thumb's diamond-cut signature on a windowpane in the house of Shakespeare's birth in Henley Street; Shakespeare's strangely unreal bust in Trinity Church and, right below, his undoubted voice cut into flat stone: 'Good friend, for Jesus' sake forbear to dig the dust enclosed here . . .!' Then came the long walk to Shottery and the high-backed settle where 'WS' may have sat with Ann, his wife; then Clopton Bridge and the Avon gently running but with no wanton boys swimming on bladders that day and, finally, our long walk home from Verney Junction Station in the evening marvelling that Miss Gwendolyn could still out-walk us. Once again we arrived at our own houses in a dream.

George Saintsbury's '*Shorter History of English Literature*', Skeat's '*Concise Etymological Dictionary*' and John's '*Flowers of the Field*' rest on my shelves today, each bearing the strong signature of this true lady. Often she would 'just run along to the schoolhouse' to see how she might quietly 'help a little there'. As the war 'ground on' - Claydon's own expression - and the long year 1917 passed into 1918, Mrs Walter grew noticeably tired and wan. So I took on more errands and the light work in her garden which she had long enjoyed - John Gamble remaining, as he put it, 'more of a vegetable man'. In the summer vacation I spent long hours in the local fields helping with the hay and corn. One such flat, featureless meadow had been named 'Wearisome' long before I tossed hay in it. At this time, too, I took time off from my homework, one evening a week in this important growing season, to hoe through my father's own root crops, he being on almost permanent 'long-time' for harvest work. It was essential to keep them swelling and sweet, for food was becoming a mighty matter for the whole nation. German U-boats were too often broaching the food convoys which naval boats like the 'Rival' stove desperately to protect. The government gave out as little information as possible on the losses at sea, but the introduction of the coarse National Loaf and 'cocoa-butter', along with dried egg of increasingly doubtful character told their own story.

One by one the village men were lost or reported missing, or were back at home 'invalided out'. Eddie Carter, the lively son of the head gamekeeper, home on convalescent leave wore four wound-stripes on the sleeve of his tunic, two from action on the Western Front and two from the vague Middle East, which he simply called 'Mespot'. He brought to enthralled listeners in the village Reading Room tales of the remarkable allurements to be enjoyed at base, namely, teeming Cairo. Claydon folk, he truly said, had seen nothing like it: with luck he might be posted back! By contrast, Archie Foskett, powerful woodsman, spent only two weeks in Flanders Fields, bringing home an arm of no further use there, which ever after would be referred to as his 'bit of luck' that got him home again in quick time. At this time, too, my young Uncle John, home on leave from the Royal Corps of Signals, might be seen standing far back in an open field practising his semaphore with a duster tied to a cricket stump, drawing to himself young learners and causing me to learn the Morse Code post haste, as something no-one should be without in war-time, 'ack-emma', or 'pip-emma'. However, for A. C. Walter there was no leave, nor hope of any, because of what he called 'busyness on the sea-lanes' so that I applied myself assiduously to my letter writing. Responses came in strange forms and never from any recognisable posting. Mine were sent to him always from the same GPO land-base. I kept to my remit, that he should hear of Claydon in its seasons, almost as if there were no war. 'It will help to keep my sanity,' he had said.

So in March or April I would write that dog's-mercury and ground-ivy were delicately out together on the road-side banks; in June and July that wild roses were scrambling over the field hedgerows alongside the making and gathering of hay and that I was helping in this in all my spare time and that fork and rake had calloused my hands, putting my handwriting quite awry. I wrote of my admiration for the wiry old men and sun-tanned women I worked with, there being now no young men or men of middle years left in the fields. The old men, lean and burnt brown, could work for hour after hour in a way I could not without exhaustion: they had the same far away look in their eyes as his seamen. A return letter of his said: 'You are growing wise in your admiration of the old men - old, but surprisingly vigorous, possessing great stamina. I watched one such on a boiling day hoeing mangolds on a Devon hillside. The toil of scores of years was stamped on his face and body, but still he was going, back bent, head forward, with the old, old swing. He had probably been there all day. I was glad to rest on a low stone wall after a walk of some five or six miles, and I am supposed to be in the prime of life!'

In November I would say that yellow leaves, or none or few hung on the dripping tree branches where late the small birds sang, or something like it, for Palgrave's Golden Treasury rarely left my pocket, and that, yet again, I was making the monthly weather calendar for the infant children, one as 'Christmassy' as I could make it, recalling how for January, 1916, he had begun the idea with a sunset over snow and flying snowballs.

His letter-writing as he explained, was done in strange places. One warm sunny afternoon, while he was on shore-leave during a re-fitting, there lay before him a field of rape, golden yellow, stretching to the horizon, like the loan-picture in the Big Room at school, he said, the one which we had ventured to copy and so capture before it was returned to base, he doing the rape, poppies and sky and I the figures. Where his field was he must not say, but it was balm, a rich and unexpected opportunity to sit and gaze, with Mother Earth comfortably steady beneath him. God knew when he would take up a paint brush again. A dash to an art gallery helped if leave permitted. Newcastle-upon-Tyne had done that a few weeks back. It had put him on an even keel again. His writing, I know, was done to get me going. I wrote one for one. 'Keep at it,' he wrote, 'you are developing a power. As for me now, big seas and HMS Rival conspire against me absolutely - no more today.' It is intensely moving to re-read his letters, each revealing the intrinsic worth of the man, each leading me towards an understanding of what I was about in setting out to be a teacher. 'He keeps us all going,' Mrs Walter said proudly. 'My last was on very strange paper - oil-stained. The best oil,' he said, 'the thickest and blackest and best. He had been ankle-deep in it - could not say where or why. Poor Arthur.' There were long delays between letters. 'Once more away on business' would be the explanation and that could mean escorting war materials round North Cape through Arctic waters to some remote Russian port, or making rendezvous in the Atlantic with American troops to be got safely to Plymouth, England, for their first footing in Europe before engaging in the horrendous 'pushes' that eventually ended the war: his word 'business' raised apprehension each time he used it as explanation for a long silence.

Not until late 1918 and the war ended did he speak of himself aboard the 'Rival'. On December 22nd he wrote: 'By the address you will notice that Xmas for me will be again on board ship. I have been reflecting tonight on my first year in the North Sea. Crowds of recollections come to mind. I certainly feel in better spirits that I did a year ago - my first impressions of the ship, of a crowd of men living in a very limited space, the hundred new experiences which met me with a rush. It left one breathless. But they are over and I feel one of the ship's company today. And I have watched the sea in all her moods - in all her beauty and in the wonderful mystery of sheer force when we have been head-on in a gale of wind and sleet. I wonder if the poet who wrote "Welcome, wild nor'easter" was ever out to sea in a real nor'easter - I doubt it.'

The war over he declared that his captain was the 'maddest ever', that through one awful night of tempest the 'Rival' was the only naval vessel in home waters not to take shelter in port. And only then, when he was safely in Claydon again, did he speak of those 'hundred new experiences', sudden and horrifying, which brought him now to be sadly less the man he was when the navy took him.

Also at the end he had written: 'Friday Nov. 22nd '18, I was in Glasgow when the news that the Armistice was signed came through. There was the usual excitement from the multitudes who flocked to the central streets of the city, but I noticed one lady in black who was greatly distressed. Sorrow is always with us in our greatest joys. I felt no desire to shout or to wave flags - feelings were too deep for noise. The Peace Conference will be soon on the way and the terrible tangle untangled. It will be the most difficult problem that civilisation has ever faced and when that is finished mankind will have the more difficult and important business of cleansing their public outlook . . . Here I suggest that you always look under the surfaces - dig deep if you would find gold. The maxim applied equally to the conduct of life. Never be led away by a superficial idea, political froth, social froth generally, but know yourself, plan a conduct of life and, when you think, worry all round the subject - no skimming surfaces. I was greatly touched by your kindly reference to my homecoming, when I "emerge from the mud" to be a human and an individual again in action and thought.'

When in mid-1919, he returned with our other surviving men it was to a village very different in mood from the one of Bossie White's national anthems, of the anticipation of what the Russian Steam-roller would do to the likes of 'Kayser Bill' and 'Little Willie' and of certainty about the inviolability of our right-little, tight-little island. They came back to drawn faces and to drawn blinds in eleven different homes, to a resigned dreariness which thoughts of peace were slow to ease. The great influenza epidemic, which seized on debilitated Western Europe the moment the war drew to its end, reached us too. Elation everywhere was muted.

Out of expediency the Government returned men from the forces in such haste that there would be no employment for most ex-Servicemen in the Claydon villages for three years. Their war gratuities mostly bought bicycles for riding in their strangely new 'demob suits' to town in order to draw subsistence money - money due, not 'dole', nor parish money, the deplored 'Parish relief', that which until recently had caused the awful word 'pauper' to appear on census and other official documents. No - they rode, they said, for their rights and if on their return home they spent more than was wise in the 'Crooked Billet' then that was their business and time too, they swore, for folk who had been 'ordered about' for years. So, sometimes, their late home-comings to a great jingle of bicycle bells and cries became a trifle riotous and a worry to the local justices of the peace, who appeared to compromise by ensuring that proved misdemeanours by returned warriors should cost no more than five shillings at the Petty Sessions. Life in the villages would never again be what it had been before 1914.

'I am fortunate. Why should I be fortunate in returning to an assured post?' asked the ex-sailorman. 'I did no more than they in the ghastly business.' But his return was timely. Mrs Walter needed immediate relief. Arthritis and distressing eye troubles, which began under the strain of continuous anxiety about him, were increasing. She had run the school quietly and effectively with courage and much saving humour. She declared that there was greater difficulty over the placing of the older boys' farm-style boots than in calling into play their varying brain-powers. I had not needed to seek out and chide a single one of them, even outsize Ronald Bowden, who already had the build of a policeman, or a coal-heaver, about him. There was intense relief all round in having A. C. Walter himself again in charge. Lona and I were now in the fourth years of our bursaries in the care of J. T. Read and by this time my family at the Weir had expanded. Three lively young brothers were a considerable constraint on my homework so, to help in the run-up to the final examinations, the 'Prelim', the upper room in the Walters' school-house was made available to me for hours of undisturbed work. My smiling hosts said: 'A long distance runner needs to work up sprinting power for the final lap.' Evening after evening, right to the final moment in June, I sat working there with a view, right before me and below me, of Farmer Tompkins's placid cattle grazing in the adjacent field, or, more often, lying in a homely group steadily chewing the cud, with a view also of the cricket practice in the far distance - a sore temptation that - until, dusk having fallen, came the voice at the stair's foot: 'Enough! Enough! - cocoa, home and bed!'

Of the looming examinations A C Walter said no more than: 'Taken out of my hands long ago. Do J. T. Read and Steeple Claydon School proud. All now lies between you, JTR, the Fair Maid of Wolverton and the all-knowing Board of Education.'

An 'Uncertificated and Recognised' Teacher at Loudwater Boys' School in 1919

By the time I became an 'Uncertificated but Recognised' young teacher at eighteen I had seen interesting, sometimes fascinating, variety in three headmasters. I was now to see variation in a fourth, for the Bucks Local Education Authority lost no time in employing me as an Uncertificated Assistant Master, untried though I was for full-time teaching. In the last days of my bursary, due to end on 31 October, 1919, I was informed that Mr T. C. Corke, Headmaster of Loudwater Council Boys' School, in the far south of the county, would expect me on his doorstep in good time before morning school on the first day of November, to fill a vacancy there. If I applied directly to him undoubtedly he would advise me about a lodging. I confess that I was startled that I would teach boys only, having known, hitherto, none other than the social mix of my Claydon schools.

I discovered from the county map that Loudwater lay beyond High Wycombe in the low land known as Wycombe Marsh and that the Thames itself was near, so it would be a strange country, should I have time to explore it. Neither J. T. Read nor A. C. Walter knew anything helpful to me about Mr Corke, or his school. Read had met him professionally, that was all, and Walter said: 'Unknown country, then. You will feel your way. Keep in touch.' I knew that I would take something of the methods of each of them with me and I was determined to employ it where I could in this new venture.

My resort to Mr Corke for help about a lodging showed him by letter to be welcoming and helpful. Mr and Mrs Hogan in the village were accustomed to taking in single gentlemen - homely people. Indeed, their daughter was teaching in the adjoining girls' school. Mr Roberts, whom I would replace, who had only now retired from the staff to settle elsewhere, had been happily accommodated with them for a number of years. Mr Hogan was a retired police officer. This knowledge suggested that the household could be assumed to be respectable and probably pleasantly quiet and well-ordered. My letter to Mr and Mrs Hogan however brought no response directly from them but, instead, from their daughter, the teacher, I supposed, who stated that twenty-five shillings a week would be asked, of course, 'in advance'. On this I laid the letter down to place this requirement against the ninety-five pounds per annum of my salary-to-be. This was sobering, but not to be compared with the disturbance of mind which ensued as I read on. So alarmingly over-welcoming were the next words that I felt for my wing-feathers, and then clutched the edge of the parental nest, for I felt myself almost on the point of being embraced. Observing my consternation, my father asked to read the letter, saying then in his well-known teasing manner, that it could be supposed that the writer was 'not yet matched'. Unfortunately, the handwriting gave no indication of the writer's age, but he thought her 'probably not very young'. These speculations failed completely to amuse me, nor did my three young brothers help, in any way, to restore my calm. My mother laughed and said: 'You will survive. Just show you were not born yesterday.' I knew that, willy-nilly, I must go to Loudwater and that now I would go with waves rather than ripples of unease: the final 'Edna Hogan' had been so painstakingly done.

Students who have been cocooned in teacher-training courses, studying History of Education, Method, Child Psychology offset by a qualm or two about teacher psychology and then projected into actual Teaching Practice, short, unreal and protected, while beset by assessments of all sorts, not least about their own suitability for a job with question-marks all over it, and who have finally entered 'the fray' – they know what is meant by being 'thrown to the wolves'. Not to the lions for swift dispatch, but to that ring of prowling creatures, eyes gleaming as the campfire sinks, who are content to bide their time. I had premonitions that something of the sort awaited me, for I could not imagine how a boys-only school would run, nor how I would adapt to it. But I knew that somchow I must show what my three headmasters and my pupil-teachers' course had done for me, so I set forth on the last day of October to seek out the Hogans in Loudwater, arriving to find the village apparently larger than even Steeple Claydon, a little scattered and level-lying and the Hogans' home a 'semi-' in a road I was tempted to designate small-town.

I had left a closely-knit family, mostly in harmony if not, like any other, continuously, in a togetherness taken for granted, but I found the Hogan family on the evening of my introduction to it to be very different. There were three adults assessing me. The head of the family elderly and non-committal certainly had the bearing of a police officer. His wife was pleasant and efficient-seeming and the letter-writing daughter, who was probably twice my age, was reflective and, perhaps, a trifle downcast. Mr Corke could not have explained to them that I was but a stripling. It was revealed to me quite soon that the Mr Roberts I would succeed in school, a bachelor of long standing, had been admirably accommodating while with them. It was reported with approval that each evening, 'as regular as clockwork', he had left them for the local hostelry, delightfully named *The Happy Union* where he had established his own corner in the 'Snug' - he would be sadly missed in *The Happy*. An obliging man, he had given no trouble.

Here, I ventured to say that I must admit to being a home bird myself, when Mr Hogan, having bent to me in order to hear this, drew himself up to speak for the first time, his few hairs groomed as if for duty and his eyes alight, saying loudly and with force: 'Mr Chapman, sir - a man is not a man if he cannot take his drink.' As he then left the room Mrs Hogan tapped her ear.

'He doesn't hear well,' she said and then, whispering to Edna: 'One of your father's bad evenings,' sighing in a way, I thought, which made clear that she was a step-mother and no more. Turning to me she said: 'He's up and he's down.'

'Always up when our Fergus comes,' Edna declared, but what that portended I could not guess.

Her father returned for supper in silence. It was a subdued gathering. She was not as expansive verbally as she had been on notepaper, but she did say that while boys and girls shared the school building I need not worry about seeing anything of her side, except that I must expect to see plenty of 'Her', this lady being her headmistress, Mr Corke's wife. Hogan maintained his silence but for the the frequent grunts which meant either please or thank you, or the reverse. My spirits sank rapidly as I drifted into exchanges with Mrs Hogan, Edna having said that Loudwater was something and nothing. Mrs Hogan said she expected I would find it, and all around, 'different'. Many of the children's mothers were full-time rag sorters in the paper mills, their men engaged in the timber yards and furniture factories, which drew from the beech woods nearby. It had been countryside when she was a girl with fields, hedges and farms - much more country then, more natural - she had been brought up a farmer's daughter herself.

I soon agreed that I would like to see, and to retire to, my room. On this Mr Hogan looked relieved and retired too and Edna said as we rose: 'It's quiet.' My bed-sitting-room was unremarkable, though the bed and chair looked comfortable enough. When Mrs Hogan left I sat on the bed, my case unopened, very much troubled. I suppose my first ever home-sickness was creeping up on me. This, then, had been the old bachelor teacher's haven after the companionship of *The Happy*? I felt sure I could detect the lingering aroma of a powerful pipe tobacco growing stale. There was a small bedside table, but for lesson preparation no surface other than the top of the dressing-chest, its drawers open and empty and waiting for me, nor was there any shelf for books. I wondered how long King Edward the Seventh and Queen Alexandra, framed and fading, had graced the opposite wall before fading from the consciousness of the whole household, Roberts included. I saw that the fireplace was carefully blocked by a screen decorated by painted roses, much over-done and that there was no evidence of the area's use for an actual fire. The words 'fully floral' came to mind as I surveyed the wallpaper. Inevitably I fell to considering this first fluttering from the family nest. I had never before given any thought to it and what it might be like, but now I knew. However, the more I thought the more certain I was that I must open my case and ensure that on the morrow I would go breast forward, never doubting clouds must break, etc., etc., hoping that bright day would cheer me and steer me to a propitious meeting with Mr Corke in his school. I could go assured, for hadn't I a fund of ideas? If I began as Mr Walter would, how could I go wrong?

Edna did not accompany me to school next morning. She said, simply: 'Just walk to the end of the road, then down the lane and you'll see the school across the Marsh.' Mrs Hogan explained further: 'She calls for her cronies,' then she added: 'It's not a marsh really. Once it was, it's just a flat common now. You can't miss the school. It stands out,' and on that I stepped out smartly in order to find it and to be early. I found the common lying low in morning mist and saw at some distance the gaunt isolated building which must be the school. Children ahead of me were approaching it. I thought as I followed them of our village school at home, of my personal brick lying secure beside the foundation-stone and of the mural,. with its climbing children, in Miss Florence Wyatt's infant room and of her in it, certainly, at that very moment busy on her preparations. I thought of the sunny morning when Lona and I arrived at the Reads' school at Steeple Claydon and of the pleasant familiarity and purpose we found there. That too would be opening to a familiar busyness. What would this strange building hold for me? As I neared it boys stood desultorily around, the girls now only briefly seen. Within minutes they entirely disappeared. But it was the building which held my attention. Stolid and ageing and brick-built, it stood large and long with a high central part to it and, in that, approached by stone steps, a great church-like door swung inwards and back. The bell-tower stood high above and all the windows were well out of reach. So, it was a school with an uneasy somewhat ecclesiastical air about it. It looked, in fact, forbidding. However I must mount the steps – the climbing brought to mind Henry Holiday's happy children once more. It appeared that the boys' entrance was by way of these steps through the doorway and into the long barren hall, where I saw above a door in the left-hand wall lettering, black, disciplined and strong, announcing 'BOYS' and on the opposite wall a similar door and, above that 'GIRLS', although I saw no girl use it at any time. Their entrance, which also I never saw, was somewhere distant in the rear.

My direction, therefore, was plain and I knocked on the left-side door. 'Never the least stir made the listeners . . .'. Why did those words leap to my mind? Well – there was no response, that was it. I waited a little, then knocked again, working also the heavy iron latch; the door opened, revealing a high wide classroom, full of desks, and a figure standing at the far teacher's table, an elderly man, who appeared not to have heard my knock, but who now looked enquiringly across at me as I stepped into the room. True to my intended briskness I advanced to him to ask, breezily, if I could be directed to the headmaster's office. 'Office? – no such grand affair here. Meet Corke if you are the new man,' was his response and he smiled and held out his hand. 'Thought I would wait for you here and save time as this will be your room,' he said. The elderly man, a slight, grey figure, was almost a replica of the reigning King George the Fifth – build, height, sober dress, the beard the same and even a little of the facial expression. Imagine that royal personage out with his 'guns' in a Scotch mist and you have T. C. Corke also in mist, or in one of the winter fogs which often lay over the Marsh, indeed over the whole area between the southern slopes of the Chiltern Hills and the Thames, on too many chilly mornings.

'Standards One and Two,' he said, 'full up, I'm afraid. I shall be on hand to start you off with them. Register here, syllabus here in the drawer, timetable on the wall. Book cupboard, readers and so on, here. Be careful with all stock, especially pen-nibs and india-rubbers. Regularly count all pencils collected in. If short of any of these things keep the class seated and send for me. But excuse me now - must get them in.' A bell was tolling dolefully overhead. 'I shall have to ask you to do this for me pretty soon,' he added and through a doorway behind us he left me. I had already taken in the dual desks, six in each of four blocks, betokening four dozen pupils and a 'front' for me, between blackboard and easel and table, no more than four feet wide.

I stepped to the near doorway to see a large, high room, very long, also packed with pupils' desks, in which two heavy green curtains were drawn fully back. Obviously, drawn forward they would separate, in a fashion, three classes of pupils. In close conversation, far in, stood two large women in sombre, pinafore-dresses, their grey hairs pulled hard back to almost identical 'buns', their stance of firm solidity. I withdrew as they perceived me, but they did not come forward: they looked very umpromising as colleagues.

Now the bell fell silent, distant whistles sounded and then a heavy tramping began, which grew in volume, its rhythm strong as the large room filled up and now, as I moved to stand by my table carefully unsmiling, my room also filled up, my complete forty-eight, with T. C. Corke at their heels. How swift was their seating, how ram-rod straight their backs, how exactly and closely folded their arms, with never a deviant. I had not seen anything like this since my earliest days in the Old School at East Claydon when 'Bossie' White's domain echoed much a T. C. Corke's had reverberated a moment ago. Corke came now to stand beside me. The nearest boys gave me fleeting glances, otherwise all eyes were fixed on him. In a sharply rasping voice he announced that this was Mr Chapman, come to be their teacher. Mr Chapman would stand no nonsense any more than Mr Roberts had. Mr Chapman had come to Loudwater School, and to Standards One and Two in particular, for hard, quiet and steady work, with Mr Corke himself close at hand - yes, very close at hand and all through the day.

'Stand up Rickaby,' he now ordered and a bright-looking boy of eight or nine years rose to his feet. 'You may as well know, Mr Chapman, that Master Rickaby thinks he's clever. Too clever by half is Rickaby. You will not be deceived by him and now, stand up Gomme and stand straight, sir! Gomme requires to be watched every minute. One foot wrong - slack work, anything - put him through to me on the instant, Mr Chapman. You can both sit now.' Several more about the c lass stood to have their propensities laid bare, while they solemnly eyed me. So, Mr Roberts had retired from this, or these, his solace his pipe and the snug of *The Happy Union*. What salves would I soon be needing? When Corke left us saying to me : 'To see to things,' he said also: 'We join for assembly and prayers in ten minutes.'

I decided that a smile would do no harm as now all eyes turned to me, with looks mildly wondering, curious, or resigned, all arms remaining grimly folded. 'Good morning, boys,' I said, as I sat at my table, giving a business-like look all round, nothing having come of my smile. The attendance-register opened before me, I dipped Mr Robert's red-ink pen into the ink-bottle, saying: 'When I call your name please stand up so that I may know you. If I pronounce your name wrongly correct me.' I made no flicker of difference about Rickaby, Gomme and the others in question as I marked them in, one by one, and all went well until finally we arrived at two Waites, twins, when the class roused on their disentanglement at the exact moment when 'Mr Corke's door' - it was ever so-called - opened wide, when, with no word from me, my class rose as one, flinging back their seats, to leap upright, breathing-in alarmingly, again as one, standing then in silence, their eyes no longer on me, but on the doorway. Even heavier leaping, and probably breathing, by the larger numbers next door completed the 'Assembly'. Corke then appeared and placed himself in the door-space for a strategic view in all directions, the silence complete throughout, not even a cough. This, then, was to be what I knew as 'Hymns', so I rose and tip-toed to a side-wall to win an approving, official smile. My lady colleagues however also stayed with their own and so were not in view.

'Today, school,' Corke began in a strong, carrying voice: 'is All Saints' Day, so our hymn for this week is *For all the saints who from their labours rest*,' the words bringing me the sudden miserable realisation that the previous evening's Hallowe'en of bobbing for apples, jolly turnip lanterns and family fun had been driven completely from my mind by my arrival at the Hogans' household. But Corke was announcing further: 'And we will learn it in the usual way, line by line. After me, then - *For all the saints who from their labours rest*,' and so there came a heavy rumbling repetition from both direction. This was done three times over when there came:

'Now Rickaby in Mr Chapman's Standard Two, stand up and let me hear those words from you.' The attribution to Rickaby of ultra-cleverness was proved by a perfect enunciation. 'I should think so, too,' Corke said, 'and don't droop, boy. Now, Mrs Saunders, your help, please - just the first line.' From somewhere behind him came a great chord and then a pounding-out of just that line, voices and piano and three times over as before. So it was done, line by line, verse one made perfect. I concluded that not until Friday could we expect a complete, or perhaps almost complete, rendering of the hymn, and I reflected further on the Christmas hymns certain to be anaesthetised and laid out for operation in this way towards perfection. This was all the 'Hymns' amounted to but for closing with the Lord's Prayer, again a heavy rumbling sound in which 'Chartneven' was perhaps taken to be an Almighty Surname?

With Corke gone and his door closed I was relieved to have my class before me, seated, watchful and expectant. First I must complete the register with the Waite brothers correctly identified and then proceed to prescribed work with a group half as large again as any I had encountered before. It can be done, as teachers know, by desk-bound methods, with little scope for individuality or movement, by step-by-step direction and a great deal done in unison. I found my observers strangely subdued - they expected that their teacher would direct every move, would give the word to begin, to take up, to lay down, to stop, to open books at page so and so, to close them as one. I suffered many misgivings as I was compelled to work this way and, further, I was astonished when Corke came to rummage in my book-cupboard behind me, saying: 'Ah - here they are,'taking up half-a-dozen grubbily thumbed infant-readers, and then: 'Carry on, Mr Chapman - do carry on. Reading group this way.' When six of my most awkward looking boys, from about the class, rose without a word to me, simply putting down my work, to form a half-circle at Corke's open doorway and begin for him a loud reading round, jerky, hesitant and nervous to a boy, about a f-airy prin-cess and ch-arm-ing pr-ince, Corke urging: 'Repeat, repeat, boy. I've broken the word up for you,' while switching observation from them to the larger room at hand and then to mine, silent over their sums. This ended and boys and books replaced, he whispered to me: 'I help in this way every day - essential to work at them and get them on. The basic test, you see, so worrying.' He was gone before I could say I might have ideas on giving him relief. At this early stage I could see a possible use of

Rickaby as a word-nourisher with a couple of slow-coaches, if I could find some taking reading matter for them. It appeared that the Council's strait-jacket of J. T. Read's scorn had a real presence here. One reading 'circle', or another, each day had a drilling. Was I, at the same time, being thoroughly overseen?

Midday brought a surprise. With the children hurrying away to their homes, I, too, made my way over the Marsh to the Hogans for midday dinner, for Mrs Hogan to say as I arrived: 'They won't be long - it's all ready,' causing me to wonder who 'they' could be apart from Edna. Meanwhile, Hogan himself entered, loudly wondering how many young sparks I had leathered already. 'Begin as you mean to go on, young man,' he said, which, of course, with reservations, is a sound enough direction. But now Edna arrived and, with her, the two lady-colleagues from beyond T. C. Corke's door. 'Mrs Saunders and Miss Bright,' Edna said, 'if you haven't met already. Mum does this for us every school day - makes us nice and homely. Good hot dinners - you'll see.'

'And no shop,' Mrs Saunders added at once. She, I supposed, was the piano-thumper and this Miss Bright immediately supported with 'No, indeed.' Both looked me over very thoroughly as they settled to the table. They could have been twins with the sameness of their iron-grey hair pulled back to identical 'buns', their dun-coloured felt hats, which they did not remove, and figures stiff, strong and almost manly. Even relaxed they looked long schooled, I thought, with Corke in moulding boys as clay. It was an awkward meal. Hogan, visibly brightened in their presence made obscure remarks which gave rise to smirking, pretended laughter, then pursed lips and hauteur, his wife saying: 'Now Tom, Mr Chapman's here,' when he turned fully on me: 'Young man, Mr Chapman, sir,' he said, 'you must expect an Irishman, whatever his company, to speak his mind, open as the day.' At once Edna came in with soothing words: 'Dad - Dad,' she said, patting his arm, 'you've got to give him time to know us,' and what lame reply I provided to that I do not recall. Her father then said: 'Suppose so - though old Roberts . . .,' but Mrs Hogan interrupted. 'Hush - hush, do,' she said, 'he's gone, so hush on him. Do us the kindness, please.' Hogan fell silent for the rest of the meal.

In the awkwardness which resulted Edna fell back on arch looks and bright tones, breaking the silence to say she wondered if, perhaps, I was missing an 'attraction' left behind in Aylesbury or Winslow, or nearer home, and if not no doubt Loudwater might help me.

Loudwater was not quite a backwater – the winter socials and dances welcomed new faces. On my becoming at once non-committal on that, silence again fell. Undeterred, she began, after a while, in a different vein – that it was a great comfort to know that we in school were all *one* still, all wicked, down-trodden 'Uncertifs' together, the two ladies signifying approval, happy to agree. I thought it advisable to nod and say nothing on that, but, sensing an opportunity, I said: 'What of the girls' side, Miss Hogan?' – this with Mrs Corke in mind, but Edna replied: '*Edna, if you please* – we're homely here, like I said. Mrs Corke do you mean? Oh, she likes to think she makes us all jump –' and now ready laughter. 'We call her "Her" when we don't call her "Madam High and Mighty".' Here Mrs Saunders said: 'The one who *really* jumps, but there, I'd better say no more,' and this to real laughter. Turning to me Edna said: 'I've got her real measure, if you want to know.'

'Just as well,' I said, learning fast and knowing when to stop. The conversation then turned to vigorously pursued local gossip. Miss Bright now became suddenly animated. I seemed to be feeling my way in a shifting fog. I grew more and more worried that I must adjust daily to propinquity of this kind. At some point I might unwittingly provide information that would evidently not go down at all well, that I planned not to remain happily 'Uncertif', but to leave them for full authentication in a college course. It could make for unhappiness. I was upon thin ice. For such treachery I could be as the wretched Rasputin in the River Neva in 1917 – I would be pushed right through it.

It was a sort of comfort to return to my class again. Would I ever know each boy as one should? Meanwhile, I had to adjust to the powerful voice of Mrs Saunders, whose class was positioned opposite Mr Corke's door where the door-panels had meekly surrendered. She harangued as much as she taught – I was sure that at times the panels vibrated. How Miss Bright contended with only the green curtain between them I could only guess. Mr Corke, surely, was somewhere beyond and immune? Frequently the voice rose to require someone named Shepherd to 'put those glasses straight'. I was amused that my boys, from familiarity, took no notice of this. But I was curious to know Shepherd, so I sought him out in play-break, when I then understood his trouble. One ear-loop of his steel-rimmed spectacles was a strip of narrow black elastic, such as went beneath the chin of most girls in order to keep the hat in place.

My classroom provided passage for all who wished to reach the headmaster, or, in reverse, for those carrying messages for him, and it appeared that the most frequent passings were going to be those of Mrs Corke. She - I knew at once it was she, or 'Her' - opened and closed the door as of right, gave the merest nod to me, but said to the nearest of my charges in passing: 'Sit up, Charlie Cook - you can't write properly like that,' giving him a sharp poke in the back for stimulus and striding on to Corke's door, still with no glance to me, opening and closing there also as of absolute right. Within minutes she returned, scanning the whole class as she went, closing the door behind her with a clang. My pupils, but for Cook and his poke in the back, had taken it quite undisturbed, showing that normality can take many forms. My impression had been of a stout well-corseted figure, the hair done high, the face unsmiling, the spectacles firmly placed. I decided that I had seen the effective head of both schools. At no time was I introduced to her. I began to develop, from all this, the uneasy feeling that I was 'goods accepted on trial', which, if proved unsuitable or unsatisfactory, would be promptly 'returned to sender', Mrs Corke having made the decision. However Mr Corke himself came to me before the afternoon session closed to restore my confidence a little by ordaining that from next morning all playground duties would be mine, and also the physical exercises of all the boys, including the older boys' organised games. The games groups would be large, he was afraid, but, no doubt, being younger, I would soon be able to improve considerably on what Roberts had managed to do for them. Knowing nothing of the boys' qualities I thought, therefore, on their quantities, saying I would do my best, Corke adding that I would have his backing, of course, without fail.

Between tea and supper at the end of the day in growing darkness I crossed the Marsh again, intending to discover something of Loudwater, for my impressions of it were extremely vague. Soon however fog came down and, not wishing to be lost, I returned with impressions mainly of muddy ways, of puzzling shop and house lights, of street lamps far apart and of a large vibrating building, less than half visible - paper or timber there? I had not found the Reading-Room, but I did suddenly come upon *The Happy Union*, where I paused, in the warm invitation of its tinkling piano, bright lighting and loud voices, to ponder on a vacant corner there where comfort and solace had been found 'as regular as clockwork' by a man more accommodating in this than I. I did not enter but found my way back to the Hogans, where also, it proved, there was music.

Mrs Hogan was preparing supper in the kitchen, Edna was absorbed in some reading and Mr Hogan sat at the table before a gramophone, his head bent to the great horn, tears trickling down his cheeks as the last notes of *When Irish eyes are smiling* dropped away.

'Ah - Mr Chapman, sir,' he said, his handkerchief to his eyes, 'you have caught me, you have. You must forgive an old man's weakness. I was from the troubled Island, you see. 'Twould be but a step back, but never shall I see it again, the old home-place. The songs melt my heart, they do. This is now my only pleasure, truly it is.' Edna looked up from her book to say: 'Not quite,' and then resumed her reading. I took a sidelong glance at her book and saw it was what was then called a novelette by a popular provider of *Ladies' Own Fiction.* When I brought my books for lesson preparation, also to the lamplight, she looked, raising her eyebrows to full height, while her father, to emphasise his rights, at once placed Count John McCormack on his turntable. So I, perforce, put my books aside to listen to that silken voice. Edna then slammed her book closed and left us. Until supper I listened with Hogan through song after song, agreeing with him that it was the wickedest thing in the world that the sweet little shamrock of Ireland was 'forbid by law to grow on Irish Ground' and that it was enough to break a true Irishman's heart, enough to make him 'rise-up, rise-up to put a few things right'. Thus, I made a little progress with him, Mrs Hogan having looked in several times, smiling and relieved, but I shed no tears myself. It was an evening I have never forgotten, ending the strangest and the longest day in my young life.

Next morning I walked to school determined to stir my class into life by ignoring the timetable. I would seek volunteers to step to the front to tell me and the class what I had only partly seen the previous evening. Gomme, the first-comer as I expected, explained that the large, busy building I had encountered in the fog was 'furniture' and that his dad was a foreman there, also that when he was fourteen he would 'go prentice' there. From several other willing informers I learned the location of the Reading-Room and a short-cut to it, also the post office. Several wished to concentrate on *The Happy Union* and, rashly, I engaged Rickaby for this, who at once introduced Mr Roberts to the scene, going at once into detail, so that I had to stop him, fearing the arrival of Mrs Corke, or Mr Corke, or both, as witnesses to his eloquence and my folly. The interlude thus was short, but it served to lighten up the whole class and to tell me much about the narrators. Set timetable work after than went cheerfully if not ideally quietly.

Playground duty helped me, for a large number of my class gathered to me, I suppose for a close view of one so different from Mr Roberts, some to pose questions.

'Was you in the war, sir?' one boy asked.

'No,' I replied, 'I was too young.'

'Lucky you, sir,' several said in chorus.

'Yes - lucky me,' I agreed and went on to say that several boys I went to school with had a rough time in the war.

'Ed's dad got killed,' a voice said, almost as a matter of fact.

'Good job when it was all over,' the first boy said and we all agreed.

With the first national celebration of Armistice Day imminent, Corke decided that 'the school must do something about it.' Consequently, *Oh God, our Help* had to be learned in the established fashion, line by line, to be sung through at the precise hour on the day, all listening then for a distant maroon to boom the beginning and then the end of a strange general silence. 'They don't understand,' Corke said to me when all were settled in their classes again, 'there is no point in trying to make them.' I mentally awarded him a point there. Again, it was a dripping wet November day. Of course, I thought of my ride of exactly year before, in weather the same, which took me to Winslow town to learn in Headmaster Pass's doorway that news of armistice had 'come through'. A good job, indeed, that it was all over, as the boy in the playground had expressed it.

I took on the formal open-air drill of the boys. Roberts had inured them to the prescribed exercises, done almost entirely in formation - no trouble there and not much fun, either. But next I must plunge with the older ones into a melée of football on the Marsh, with numbers to make at least four elevens, no goal-posts, no marked playing area, two footballs only and heaped coats to mark the goals. Only I possessed football boots, joining alternately in two separate rough-and-tumble games, to be regarded as a wonder, numbers gathering to see if I had prowess. 'Mr Roberts never, ever, played, sir,' they said, 'too old. He let us pick sides and then lit his pipe - couldn't play with his pipe on, could he, sir? Blew his whistle for us to start and to stop at the end. Always said if it was a goal or not - no argument. Used to stand under that tree, sir, with his coat on and his collar turned up and his bowler hat on. Do you play for a team, sir? Wally Turner's dad plays for the Wanderers, don't he, Wally?'

'For Wycombe Wanderers?' I said, 'He must be good.'

'Course he is,' came in Wally, 'he'll get me a trial. Wish we had a proper ground and some goal-posts, sir.'

'So do I,' I said fervently – 'for a start, though, who can bring balls of any sort for next week for dribbling and passing practice?' Having bought the boots I could not afford to buy them a third ball. It passed for the 'Organised Games' printed on the timetables. Corke could never visit us, could never arrange to see us 'in play'. 'Too much on,' he said, but he was thankful that now we had just what the boys needed! I sighed and raised the matter of goal-posts and perhaps another ball.

'Funds – funds,' he replied, sharply, 'with funds we'd be all right for all manner of things – perhaps a ball' and that was that. Could Wally Turner's dad help? Wally said his dad could not come to see us play as he was working, but Wally played in football boots thereafter and, furthermore, supplied two leather practice balls, well-used by the Wanderers. With giving the older boys just what they needed, I had to balance the knowledge that Mrs Saunders was released to harangue mine. They were regularly subdued on my return to them. Moulding could not begin too early – 'a chance,' she stated, 'to get them into line before they come to me' – a thought she put quite openly to me.

Christmas was approaching fast, so in the morning assemblies Mr Corke, Mrs Saunders and the school beat out four verses each of *Once in Royal* and *Wild Shepherds Watched* –, all words to be written out in dictation periods, my boys showing, nevertheless, that 'wild' for 'while' remained general amongst them when in song. As relief from the heaviness in this approach to Yuletide I set about teaching my boys *Here we come a-wassailing among the leaves so green.* It had to be by the required, laid-down, Tonic Sol Fah Method. I had found them pretty agile on the modulator hung on the wall. Evidently Roberts had taken them thoroughly up and down it, even to the half-tones, but they seemed to have no repertoire of songs from it. Gomme, who was proving himself daily ubiquitous as alleged, volunteered that 'we did try to do *Come Lasses and Lads* – but Mr Roberts gave it up, so we did *Hearts of Oak* instead.' Well, it is a bouncy air for the method. As for my 'leaves so green.' mastered at last by Tonic Sol Fah, they resolved me from that time to go for Staff Notation only for the rest of my days.

The lesson timetable had to be strictly followed. In the 'Composition' period, say, the Headmaster would look in to see what we might be doing, staying awhile should it be oral and the topic perhaps 'Loudwater in the Rain' and the results a communal effort, entered by me on the blackboard. Often he would be 'on hand', as he called it, for a change of lesson. My ideas for unusual poems to be put to the class could be introduced only in 'Recitation'. With Christmas nearing I told them of Thomas Hardy's fantasy about the cattle kneeling on Christmas Eve and then spoke to them *The Oxen*. It caused a wonderment good to see. 'Oh, yes,' I said, 'I keep poems I like in my head, all my favourites.'

'Can't we learn it, sir?' they asked. In little time they took it from me - 'to keep in *your* heads,' I told them.

I think that wherever Mrs Corke trod on school premises the worrying matter of control was uppermost in her mind. Probably she thought that the working-together which I allowed, even encouraged and arranged more and more and the fact that my phalanx was never completely quiet in the so-called quiet periods, would build up, at some point soon, to an inevitable explosion. So, often after she had passed through, Mr Corke would visit us to take a long walk round the class, which then fell into deep quietude, as he said: 'All exercise books open and at your best page in each book. It is all I want to see.' He was helping, of course, giving support, but because I concluded that he was prompted by Mrs Corke, it rankled. I knew myself that, apart from occasional bright, promising moments, I was not achieving enough. They were unwittingly hampering me. The methods of A. C. Walter, J. T. Read and some of 'Bossie' White seemed far away: I could venture on them only with care and but little. I rarely returned to my lodging with any anticipation of pleasure to come, unless from the book I was reading and would take to bed with me - I was leaving nothing of Thackeray unread at that time. Many evenings between tea and supper I tramped the darkened ways of Loudwater thinking furiously. However, once, with Christmas near, I had some reward. Somewhere far off in the winter gloom boys' voices were singing: *Here we come a-wassailing among the leaves so green. Here we come a-wandering so fair to be seen —*'. I stopped at once and craned to listen. On they piped: *God bless the master of this house, God bless the mistress too and all the little children that round the table go – Love and joy come to you —*' and so on right through. They had it complete.

Lunch-times at Hogans' table seldom went better than the first. My lady colleagues made few approaches to me. The separation of the two sides, schools, if you wish, was so complete that, apart from Edna, I recall none of Mrs Corke's teachers. Girls were so little seen that at times I toyed with a strange fancy - that Loudwater suffered from a severe imbalance of the sexes, our boys having few, if any, sisters. So how was Loudwater Council Girls' School composed?

Mrs Hogan was a most able provider of hot meals, as Edna had stated, and was a competent landlady. I developed a sympathy for her, because Hogan was a man of variable moods, over-weening in some lunch-hours, awkwardly silent in others and ever ready to make plain that I was extraneous, a poor substitute for my admirably accommodating predecessor and there was a further problem. He was fond of the whisky bottle and over-indulged with his son Fergus on the weekend visits to the house, much to Mrs Hogan's embarrassment.

Darker mornings, darker days and very dark evenings led us to Christmas week. I now knew quite well every boy in my class, by nature and potentiality, especially the lively ones, who daily grew more lively. So I sought out something by John Alexander Chapman, poet but no relation, who made a Christmas poem which I knew would 'take well'. It was inspired by the stained-glass window in Thaxted Church, in Essex, in which on Christmas Morning the country creatures announce the Birth of Christ. The boys liked Hardy's *The Oxen* and recited it to me at the touch of a button, so I set about teaching them this, since it has delightful similarities. With the help of my scraps of Latin translated for them on the blackboard, the class could form groups to be the crowing cockerel, the lowing bull, the quacking ducks, the solemn raven and the plaintive lambs. It took their fancy at once. With the timetable suspended during the last days of term, we would make a small project of it. Our unusual sounds soon caused Corke to look and then withdraw stroking his beard and smiling a little. It was agreed that I would do the narration and they the creatures in groups in unison and that we would have it quite ready by Friday, breaking-up day.

Furthermore, a personal, even blissful, lightness had energised me. I had received a letter from A. C. Walter, who in my absence had succeeded J. T. Read as head of Steeple Claydon School, saying that if I thought it would be of advantage to me to help my saving to go to College, Miss Payne was about to leave him and her two first and second year classes might be available to me, if I would like to think about it - we could decide in the holiday, so, what about it? What about it, indeed! All around me that day must surely have noticed in me a cheerfulness not seen before.

I spoke to no-one about this letter and set about bringing *Christus natus est* to full production. Corke looked in again, stayed to listen and said: 'Well done. Keep at it boys. I think the quackers enjoy it most.' and then left actually smiling. In the last afternoon Mrs Corke passed through as we were enjoying the second, or third, run-through that day and on her return stood to listen to a full presentation - to the shrill '*Christus natus est*' of my chanticleers, to the booming '*Ubi? Ubi?*' of Rickaby amongst the bulls, looking round and asking, 'Where?' - to the '*Quando – quando?*' of my ducks, asking 'When?', Gomme in the lead there - to the croaking '*Christus – Christus* 'of the deep-voiced ravens and the plaintive '*In Bethlehem*' of my lambs, they having been coaxed to that part. I cared not, for I had the bit between my teeth, emboldened by my letter and by the knowledge that by supper time I would see my home in Claydon. She waited until the end, turning then to the door saying: 'Good gracious,' and as she raised the latch, 'Thank you, young man,' which were the only words she had ever addressed directly to me, so far.

I should have told Mr Corke of the letter before leaving. Had I been older I certainly would have done. He could not know how desperate I was for home, to have what was proposed made certain, to be engaged fully in my Claydon sort of schooling. It was settled with A. C. Walter before the New Year. I wrote to Mr Corke at once, explaining that living at home in preparation for going to college was the compelling reason for transfer, but I received no reply, concluding that Mrs Corke had imposed a veto. I returned to Loudwater to see the month of January 1920 through to a very cool reception. By leaving so I was putting the school to great trouble. The loss of the so steady, so utterly reliable and experienced Mr Roberts had still to be made up. 'However,' Corke continued, 'a pity this - a great pity, because I could have made something of you, given time. Several times I had thought it.'

Edna wasted no time in informing me of what Mrs Corke had to say. It seemed she was a little disappointed. It seemed that any faint hope she had of me before Christmas was snuffed out. I was emboldened to say that necessity is a hard driver and kept to myself thoughts on unofficial headmistresses of boys' schools. Thereafter Mrs Corke displayed no interest in me. I would have liked some acknowledgement that my boys were mostly quietly busy when she passed through. Corke himself looked in less often. As to the boys, who next would be thrust upon them? Who would activate rather than suppress the likes of Gomme and Rickaby?

From my final spell in Loudwater Boys' School I cherish one unexpectedly happy afternoon. At two o'clock, the afternoon session just begun, my door quietly opened to bring Mrs Corke tip-toeing straight to me at my table. Agitated, pale, even tremulous, she whispered unnervingly close to my ear: 'Have you closed your register? Make sure. HMI on the premises - with poor Miss Hogan now. Tell Mr Corke for me at once - I must fly,' and as well as physically she was able she flew back to her realm, while I, so to speak, flew to Mr Corke, spreading alarm through two more ample bosoms, Corke saying: 'Carry on as usual, surely,' for which I mentally accorded him another good point. At around three o'clock my door opened again and in stepped E. C. Streatfield, to our instant shared pleasure. A supporter and admirer of A. C. Walter's work during and after the war, admirer also of the Reads, he had been a warm encourager of Lona and me as beginner pupil-teachers. Tall, strikingly blue-eyed, he was a man with whom children were easy at once. My boys turned instantly to smile openly on him. When, later, I told them that he was a well-known cricketer who had helped to make Surrey the County Cricket Champions for three summer seasons running, they said it proved he was the right sort of man to be a school inspector. For children, invariably, he had something interesting, often quite unexpected, up his sleeve. In East Claydon School he said that on his way to them through the village he had heard the sweet song of a very small bird. What could it be? He then cleverly whistled the delicate notes of a golden-crested wren. Now, ignoring my register, syllabus, timetable and my laid out lesson-notes, he said that when crossing the Marsh he had seen a flock of strange birds, like thrushes, but with dull waistcoats, not the bright yellow with brown spots he had expected to see. Had we seen them? What were they? - Did anyone know? I said I thought I knew, but he said: 'Hush, Mr Chapman, please. I think they were field-fares come down from the North. Find out their other name see who is first to tell Mr Chapman.' He turned then to find Mr Corke's door, saying quietly to me: 'What a family!' and then, as he passed through to the next room, 'See you soon at Claydon.' I wondered what Mrs Corke thought of field-fares, if he had introduced them there; and I thought also of what he had made of Edna in action and then of what, in the evening, she would say of him. Inevitably my imminent leaving brought on some levity of thought about Corke's shaken lady. I was not unhappy that she might flutter and quiver right to the closing bell, until E. C. Streatfield HMI was safely off the premises.

I nursed a hope that his visit to Loudwater might bring a review of the school authorities' narrow provision here, that it might approximate more nearly to that already envisaged in the Claydon and other village schools. With J. T. Read and A. C. Walter strongly in my mind and their concern for the poor and under-privileged, an insistent anger had mounted in me at Loudwater, which, put into plain words, could very well be: 'No-one must say that this is enough for the children of my hard-working timbermen and women rag-sorters.' T. C. Corke may have felt the same but, if so, I never heard him say so directly. He was hampered on a grand scale. 'Funds - funds!' he had exclaimed, regarding footballs and goal-posts and then, 'With funds we'd be all right for all manner of things.' He could well have mentioned also overbearing numbers and out-dated premises. He had to do the best he could with what was laid down for him and with the incalculable help, such as mine, made available to him. When I left on my last day with him he said he wished me well and, again, that he could have made something of me, given time. Yes - he had felt it on several occasions, especially recently. 'By the way,' he said, with a half-smile and stroking the small, pointed beard, 'I shall remember that not once did you put a boy through to me, not even young Gomme.'

'I was determined on that,' I said.

My step was light as I crossed the Marsh for the last time. Looking back I saw the school standing isolated as ever, but clear in the late January sunshine - so often it had lain in mist, or fog. I felt no regret on leaving it, so strangely conceived and used as it was. As for my forty-eight boys, mortals ever resilient, they would adapt to what must follow as they long had to Roberts and then briefly to me. The bright spirits I recall best from my highway of a classroom enliven my thoughts even today.

As for my sojourn with the Hogans with the addition of Mrs Saunders, of 'the voice' and Miss Bright for lunch, not forgetting Fergus on Saturdays, I agree with my father who upon my expanding on them, observed: 'Experience - it's all experience. Learn by it - it takes all sorts to make a world.'

The first school-day of February, 1920, saw me cycling at speed on the familiar route to Steeple Claydon, familiarity happily enhanced by the presence of John Ladyman, the stout roadman, on his Middle to Steeple Claydon stretch, who, taking his time, as ever, leaned on his shovel to call as I passed: 'Been away somewhere, have you?' In reply I joyously rang my cycle-bell and pedalled faster than ever.

From Claydon to Culham
1920–1923

Back at Steeple Claydon School I found that A. C. Walter, after his bitter experiences in the First World War, from which he never fully recovered, had nevertheless plunged straight back into the personal teaching and leadership I recalled so well. He had invaluable help in 'the most important job in the world' - his words - from my cousin Lily Chapman who had been, ten years before, my own teacher-of-teachers. Now she was at home again to care for her invalid father and so became an unexpected boon and colleague to me.

It was good to see A. C. Walter's ideas and innovations complementing those I had come to admire in J. T. Read and to know that the village's loss of him would be made up in quick time. Indeed, it was not long before a respected and thoughtful Steeple Claydon man, standing at the top of Challoner's Hill in that up-and-down village, could say to me: 'What sort of a man have they brought us now? The school's a good furlong below us - now isn't it? Yet I've heard his voice from this spot, clear as a bell, a-singing to the children, pretty every word plain to be heard.'

It was sad that after something like that the voice would go silent and the powers fail for a while, the singer having fallen into what he designated one of his low periods.

'Exigency of war, they called it,' he would say. 'I was caught in an exigency.' Only rarely would he dwell on his war years, mainly to say that destroyers were fearfully uncomfortable fighting machines, being built for speed, their plating almost impossibly thin - giving a rough ride; also that the port of Archangel in northernmost Russia quite failed to live up to its name and that having been fated to go on northern convoys only, he had seen enough of the midnight sun, though, conversely, he had been glad of a full mid-night moon on occasion. Once only did bitterness creep in: 'When the Americans chopped us in two, as they went through they took the good ship's doctor with them, the very man needed in all the horror and turmoil - that's war.'

Recovered, he would be again the wound-up spring of a man we knew, urgently making up for lost time. With examples of his and my cousin's skills daily before me and of the generous advice and guidance they gave me, I was doubly grateful, for as my teaching went on I rapidly learned that I was but a fledgling helper of the boys and girls assigned to me. To be in charge of a whole class, teaching all subjects, including physical education to officially prescribed tables, organised games and music with no 'free' periods for preparation - leave alone personal refreshment, or recovery - was far different from the periodic supervised teaching practice of my pupil-teacher years.

How did Lily Chapman achieve quiet busyness in her classes while my likeable charges were ever restless? Neither she nor A. C. Walter, nor our other experienced colleagues, seemed at any time baffled - and truly that is the word - as I was by my ginger-haired Emma Richards, of Standard Three. I liked Emma, admired her quick intelligence and confident airs and spirit, but she could cock her eye at me with half a smile, and sit down to her work more or less how, or when, she pleased. Firmly adjoined by me: 'Please go to your place, Emma,' she would do so only lingeringly. Her work did not suffer, but my authority did. In the next hour, before either of my elders, she would sit the meekest of lambs. This was a mystery which the Master of Method, in my training college, a year or so later, quite failed to solve for me, since he appeared to know nothing of bafflement of any kind. But later, another of my headmasters was more helpful. With amusement in his eye, he offered advice to young male newcomers to his staff in his London school: 'In mixed classes always begin, and then continue, with more firmness with the girls than with the boys - boys alone, not an ounce of trouble. Mind you, say nothing of this before any lady.'

A. C. Walter would look in on us occasionally and say: '*Em-ma!*' and she would settle at once and if Lily Chapman came to my room on any matter Emma would slide to a seat almost imperceptibly. However, in the last hour one Friday afternoon I began reading to the class *Lorna Doone*. From the moment of old John Fry's arrival at Taunton School to take young John Ridd home to Plover's Barrows Farm, Fry finding it so very difficult to reveal the dreadful reason for his coming, Emma sat with her head in her hands, quite still, until the final bell. Still she did not move. As the class moved out to go home, slowly she rose and then paused at my table: 'Please,' she said, 'only on Fridays for this book - only on Fridays?'

'I'm going to find more time for it, Emma,' I said, 'in the week.'

'Oh, yes, please,' she said and almost skipped as she left. Had I found the beginning of a solution?

Often after school the smiling headmaster would say: 'Teaching - an art or a science?' and once: 'Teachers continually, as a matter-of-course, ask questions of children, knowing themselves the answers. Those who don't question themselves *AS A MATTER-OF-COURSE* are no teachers at all.' He saw me through eighteen months of valuable first-hand experience and self-questioning, so that I left for college well primed at least with questions on how to bring out the best in young people in their infinite varieties, taking him as exemplar.

* * * *

It was 1920, and I was eighteen when A. C. Walter once more stepped in with help at an important moment. I must go to college if I was to become a worthwhile builder of young minds, as Schoolmaster White had put it to me in 1915. In school vacations I had worked long hours in the hay and corn to make it possible, saving 'to the last penny', as

Culham Diocesan Training College near Abingdon in the early 1920s – the Terrace. Photograph: Culham Educational Foundation

Claydon would explain it, with the steady support of my parents who could not help me as much as they wished because I had by then become the eldest of a much enlarged family.

'Culham Oxford Diocesan for Men it must be,' A. C. Walter declared, 'and will be if we apply early.' The college prospectus spoke of an annual intake of around fifty men. 'Culham is a little more than forty miles distant - you will save travel costs. Good men have trained there,' were his reassuring words. With the help of a Joint Grant and Loan from the Bucks County Local Education Authority; a written reference from A. C. Walter (which quite made me blush); a copy of my baptismal certificate and a satisfactory medical report from a named doctor in Winslow, I was accepted for the years 1921 to '23, if I would present myself at the college on a date in late September, 1921. The prospectus told me that the principal, Canon A. R. Whitham, and a dedicated staff welcomed committed men to their successful Church of England establishment of much character, set up in 1852 by the renowned founder, Bishop Samuel Wilberforce, whose conviction and foresight bore fruit wherever Culham men taught. There followed a forthright assertion - that 'Ground in yonder social mill we wear each other's angles down'.

Culham College lay in a bend of the Thames, near Abingdon and south of Oxford. Though it was not far distant from Claydon, reaching it, accompanied by a tin trunk, would not be easy. However, I set forth in light spirits on the appointed day, for to cover the first stage of my journey, the two miles to Verney Junction LNWR Station, I had ready help. Young ever-cheerful Lionel Warner of the village enlisted Polly, the farm donkey, so that in her handy small cart, my trunk beside me, Lionel and I travelled very pleasantly, singing most of the way, Polly responding daintily and readily to our melody. So we arrived in good time, after as happy a ride as any I remember.

Lionel, deciding to see me on my way, was puzzled that I lingered for a while in the empty, echoing waiting-room and more puzzled still when, in response to his questioning look, I replied: 'Red ink, Lionel - miles of it,' but then, with a clatter, the train drew in. The London and North Western Railway carried me gently to Oxford, where my trunk and I must find the Great Western Railway Station for Didcot and then Culham.

There at around three o'clock I stood amidst fellow new arrivals while my trunk went to a great waiting van and knowing men were moving off. Following these knowledgeable ones I felt a hand on my arm as a voice said: 'Some say *Good Old Bucks*. Hubert Chapman are you? I'm George Scull, Bucks also - senior man appointed to seek you out and ease you in. Call me Napper if you like, everybody does. I'm ex-army.' Napper was of sturdy farming stock - 'Amersham way,' he said, looking much more farmer than teacher, or student. In his genial company we joined the walking groups with a purposeful stride.

'It's exactly one mile station to college,' Napper said, 'PE types claim to run it in five minutes.' We were on the Dorchester, Wallingford, Abingdon to Oxford road, with expanses of flat, clean-shaven corn-land on either side.

'It's arable country this way,' Napper commented. 'At home we are mixed, same as you, I expect - more interesting. All the same, look back and you'll see Wittenham Clumps and away to the left, near, but out of view from here is the Thames. Also,' and this with a grin,'if you are into politics and heavily concerned with matters of state, H. H. Asquith lives handy - Sutton Courtney is on our left a bit further on.'

Around us were the jocular tones of senior men returned from the 'Long Vac' and the tentative ones of newcomers such as I. With the college not yet in sight, I said: 'I'm keen to see the building itself, quite a structure I'm told.'

'Yes,' Napper agreed. 'Soapy Sam built it to last as you will see.'

'Soapy Sam?' I queried, 'Oh yes, the Bishop. Are all you seniors from the Forces?'

'Mostly,' he replied, 'plus a small group of older "Uncertifs" here to get qualified in one year and there is to be a contingent from West Wales, a mixed bunch, I should think, of war-time reserved ex-shipwrights.'

'And added to them,' I said, 'a group of greenhorns like myself, making altogether a very mixed company.'

'All because of the war,' Napper agreed, 'all because of 1914–18. They say,' he continued, 'that the 1914 men volunteered, almost to a man, to join the Oxford and Bucks Light Infantry and the college stood empty until Whitham opened it again last year for us - except that some college women from London took refuge in it for a time when London was bombed. The Prinny calls that "the sorry invasion". He spent the war years at his living in East Ilsley, way back in the Downs - some say to work out detailed regulations to keep us all in order.'

'Regulations such as?' I queried, but Napper said, 'You'll know soon enough and now, look, through the trees, the college.' Hurrying now I saw that the Bishop had gone for stolidity in stone and a semi-ecclesiastical impressiveness which would persist long beyond my brief encounter with it.

Standing well back on rising ground it had a straight tree-lined drive for approach. There was at the moment a warm autumn sunlight flooding it, but the building, heavily monastic in its conception, appeared ready to frown at any moment, so that, inevitably, as we turned to enter the drive, I recalled for a second poor Sue Brideshead in 'Jude the Obscure' and the establishment from which she fled, but it was a fleeting thought and we went on.

'It's no home from home,' Napper said. 'One of those small high windows looking straight down on us is mine. Don't ask me which - I don't ever know, they are so exactly the same.'

'Anyway you have a lordly view," I assured him. As the drive led us to stone steps rising to a great open doorway in the frontage, I was cheered to see long beds of flaming snapdragons at the foot of the walls and autumn-leaved climbers in haphazard patches above. We mounted the steps. Napper nodded left saying: 'Prinny's quarters,' next, pointing right to a building which was clearly the college chapel with a row of dark cypresses impassively alongside it, he said: 'Twice a day we have to be there against a shilling fine for absence - there's a rota of Juniors now, praises be, for the organ-pumping. How are your muscles?'

With these unelaborated matters to muse upon, I accompanied him into the crowded entrance-hall, pressing, with others, to the notice board, which proclaimed: 'Information and guidance for new men'. But Napper said: 'You can come back to this. Let's first find your abode, or, shall we say, nest?'

We turned to mount the wide stone flight for the dormitories. 'You are in Pandy,' Napper said, 'Number 16.' The facing rows of wooden cubicles, called Pandemonium, were each open at head-height and below well over ankle height, while the floor running beneath them was of smooth comfortless bare stone. Halfway along was Number 16, my name in the card-slot on the door.

'Enter,' Napper said, 'here are your comforts, or will be shortly when your trunk is delivered to your door. Observe your bed-linen of stout tent canvas. Feel also the straw mattress pounded by steam hammers to the required solidity.' Gingerly I felt both, taking in around us a cleverly contrived austerity.

'Is yours like this, Napper?' I enquired.

'Exactly,' he replied.

I moved then to the narrow window to look down on stone-built cloisters around a green garth and, beyond and opposite, rows of unwinking windows like mine. 'Paradise matching Pandemonium - fair enough. I'm in Major. You saw it from the drive, or may have done. I'll leave you now. You will get all the information you need below.' 'Many thanks, Napper,' I said, 'you have done me proud.' 'For good ole Buck's sake,' he answered as his footsteps echoed away.

Around me, to banter, sighs and laughter men were discovering, or re-discovering their flimsy abodes, so I emerged to savour the scene. At once a brisk smiling neighbour approached saying: 'Are you new too? I'm Granville Jackson. Where are you from? Let's explore this astonishing place together.' This was the bright son of a Wiltshire headmaster, my co-mate through the course, later friend and colleague in first teaching posts in London and he and his family friends for life. 'Let's begin with the information board below,' I responded. The main requirement there was that all new men should be seated in the Junior Lecture Room by five o'clock sharp, where detailed instructions and advice would be given by D. J. Webber, Junior Monitor. 'There's time,' said Granville, 'let's do a quick survey.' This revealed that the lecture-room shared one side of the cloister, the Senior Lecture Room another and beyond that stood severe stone portals - 'Staff, I reckon,' Granville observes, 'or dining hall, perhaps?'

In a separate block beyond was a large general Common Room, with laboratories above and standing a little apart, with playing fields and tennis courts adjoining, were the brick-built single-storey 'Houses of Parliament', as Granville and I together designated them, outside lavatories where none ever dallied for debate or speech to astound the nation. 'Hm,' we agreed together, 'I expect we'll get used to it.' We walked on to assess the length of the main building, finding the Monitors' own Common Room on the way and then the chapel - beyond that corn fields. 'All solid stuff,' Granville said as we turned. 'Do you observe that every senior-looking chap about the place carries a cushion under his arm?'

'Ominous,' said I, 'SOS home, I think. Let's now find the Junior Lecture Room for rest and mental refreshment.'

There we soon found the reason for cushions, for we sat at single desks in files, finding the seats as polished as glass and hard as only ancient oak can be. The desk lid before me was informative. 'Bongo 87–89', it said incisively, as simply did 'JJW' and 'Spike' of '60–63', the latter faint, almost smoothed away. The room was high and wide, the windows quietly ecclesiastical. An ample rostrum, huge blackboard behind, awaited our Junior Monitor.

As a bell in the cloisters shakingly announced the hour he arrived, an affable well-built youngish man who stood high to take us all in, saying then that he was D. J. Webber and that as Junior Monitor he would be ours and we his 'for the duration'. So we would begin with a roll-call. Afternoon private study here, supervised by his good self, would always be preceded by roll-call. 'Well now,' he said, perusing his sheet, 'a clear *adsum* from every man, if you please—' and thus it was throughout our Junior Year. We were gathered, he then said, to be reminded of the arrangements imperative to the day-to-day running of the college. The Principal held himself *in loco parentis* to every man accepted for training and had himself formulated guidance to be followed without question, so everyone please note:

(i) Morning chapel. 8am compulsory, as also evening chapel on Sundays.
(ii) Afternoon and evening private study here Monday to Friday compulsory.
(iii) The Principal's and all his staff lectures here compulsory.
(iv) Access to dormitories strictly forbidden between 8am and 9.30pm daily.
(v) Extensions - the prescribed times of freedom to leave the college - to be respected absolutely, as that all local licensed premises placed out of bounds and no alcoholic liquors to be brought into college, both against heavy penalty.
(vi) Association with 'outside persons' beyond the college and with domestic staff within utterly forbidden.
(vii) Furthermore, no 'female person' to be invited, or brought, into college without the Principal's direct sanction.

Here our D. J. Webber, Monitor, paused because a general murmuring through the room was broken by a voice, away to the rear, quietly saying: 'My God.' Ignoring this Webber went calmly on to

The Chapel of Culham College in the early 1920s.
Photograph: Culham Educational Foundation

The Dining Hall of Culham College in the early 1920s.
Photograph: Culham Educational Foundation

say: 'You are free now till chapel at seven to meet the Principal. Be here again at 9.30am tomorrow for written tests to decide on study-groups.' We rose to leave in a great murmuring, Granville at my ear saying: 'Poor old Herman Munday – I know him a little. He got himself engaged to the sweetest girl only last week.'

The dining hall, entered at six, led off the far side of the cloister and appeared to impinge on what Napper had called the Canon's quarters and certainly within was an impressive high-table. We stood at heavy wooden tables, each taking eight men with a Senior at the head. A precentor asked the Lord to bless what His bounty had provided and we sat to see that it was thick slices of bread and margarine and one slice each of plain cake, although Seniors had with them items of their choice. Tea in china cups was brought to us from a side-table by tall Plato, an expressionless waiter-like figure, who stood quietly by as Seniors reached for and took up all the new cups to strike off their handles with spoons, knives, anything handy, making a delightful tinkling through the hall as the fragments danced on the tiled floor. This done the established handle-less cups were now matched, poor apologies for the beer-mugs which no longer graced our boards.

Amazed and amused we beginners learned that the Canon had come to his principalship some years before the war to find that good English ale was brought to table as it had been for decades. Though he frowned upon it he tolerated it until 1914 and the war, which, it seems, had provided him with the opportunity to ponder in his East Ilsley rectory on a change to be implemented upon the re-opening. This change from beer to tea was mightily deplored, especially by the drinking men who came to him from the Forces – if there was to be beer in mugs no more, then tea-cups must be rendered as mug-like as possible. Half-way through our meal from someone in the rear of the hall rose a cry: 'There is *no* bad beer,' which cry was to be heard at opportune and, more often, inopportune moments about the college throughout my course. The Canon had touched a very tender spot in his student body.

Tea done, we were free to amalgamate in the Common Room for a while. There I saw what a mixed company we were. Grey-haired ex-servicemen, one with a limp, several with wound-stripes, clustered in the groups they would always favour. Napper found me three other Bucks men for friendly exchanges, as new men in growing confidence revealed their origins and hopes to one another. Someone wound up a gramophone which jiggingly played *Baby Tank*, and set several pairs solemnly dancing.

Chapel at seven o'clock assembled the complete company in strange contrast, sitting, for the most part comfortably, in the close oaken pews as the student organist set about pulling everyone in with power. No such scene had been known there since Culham men had gone to war in 1914. In a church setting established over long years, I found the plain-song peculiar and the nearby precentor startling. There was everywhere a quiet expectancy and then, to a note of triumph from the organ, the Canon, darkly clad and fully robed entered to the wavering words of a psalm, robustly half spoken, a counter tenor leading. A confident yet slight figure, he appeared to me to be well past middle age. Grim features, beneath short, white hair and daunting eyebrows, broke a little into a faint smile of satisfaction as from his podium he gave us a full, slow survey awaiting the organ's dying tones to accord him silence.

That given, he said: 'Pray be seated,' and then that it was a glory that this second year of opening should bring together at last a body of dedicated men to fill the revered building as it was ever meant to be filled and had been year after year since the days of 'our great Founder' until halted by the tragedy of war. Culham now could rise again - no Principal of Culham, he declared emphatically, could ever have had in his care a student-body as varied in experience and gifts as we who now sat before him. It was a blessed privilege which he would honour hour by hour, and day by day.

'But now,' he said, pursing his lips and again looking us over, 'to immediate matters, and foremost the smooth running of the College which will require regular attention to all notices and readiness to conform to the minimum of regulations laid down after long thought. 'And here,' he said with a real smile, 'the ex-servicemen with us today will recall an ever-present injunction - *Read company orders*. He would not dwell on them now - it had been a long day of travel for many men, he well knew, but company orders were about the college to be read and pondered over. We then closed standing for the hymn of his personal choice: *The Church's one Foundation*.

As we filed out Napper came to me, saying, 'Finding your way around? Sent home for a cushion? The Prinny enjoyed making an occasion of it, didn't he? - Dreamed of it for four or five years, I suppose, text pre-ordained.'

Granville and I explored further, especially the library by sanction of the two Monitors, then joined our new acquaintances in the

Common Room which was growing more animated every minute, the gramophone quietly persisting, as so often it would with the *Air on the G-string*.

Supper at 9.30 comprised thick slices of bread, cheese and cocoa, the cheese so unpalatable that it was known as 'Old Stinger' - it never changed. The cocoa was scalding hot, thick and dark and only faintly aware of milk and sugar. Some dipped bread in the cocoa, few appeared to touch the cheese and, quite soon, men slipped quietly away. This supper collation and response to it stayed the same throughout my stay - a persisting austerity from the war.

I too slipped away, for now it was permissible, as Granville wryly said, 'To go to roost.' Our trunks awaited us. Obeying instructions I emptied mine and placed it for re-collection - it would not appear again until July 1923. My belongings looked sadly meagre as I prepared for a testing of the bed-linen and the mattress below by lying on them. Gazing for a while on the wide ceiling above me I turned to dwell on some of the more astonishing moments of that long day and, puzzling a little on the voices and movements of my near neighbours, surprisingly I 'fell on sleep', feeling no discomfort from the bed-linen whatsoever. I had encompassed an introduction impossible to imagine while I was awaiting it. I retain it still complete in memory in all its strangeness and unexpectedness as truly momentous to my young hopes and desires; and the years have dimmed no iota of it.

Next morning saw me again at my desk in the Junior Lecture Room, the lid well padded against the past activities of such as 'Bongo 87–89' and 'Spike 60–63'. All subjects would be tested so no doubt I would be revealed as scholastically completely one-sided, blatantly reflecting the imbalance I developed under J. T. Read of Steeple Claydon School. However, fortunately, I did well enough to be recommended to the Advanced Courses in English Literature and Geography, while apparently proving that my History was of good quality and my General Knowledge what A. C. Walter would have required it to be, for I gained top marks in a strange miscellany of questions, one of which supposed one might know that the newly-formed League of Nations comprised fifty-seven members of sorts. But inevitably I joined small groups at the very bottom of the Science and Mathematics lists, my fellows eyeing me with amused wonder.

Advanced 'Eng. Lit.' took me next day to the study of the jolly Reverend R. Trevor Davies along with Frank Dann, an Oxford native; Emrys Davies of Bargoed, South Wales and Albert Wellman from

The Junior Lecture Room of Culham College in the early 1920s.
Photograph: Culham Educational Foundation

somewhere in London, to learn that our work would be covered in seminar there and that the Principal in his study would help too. This was exciting. I am now unclear on most that absorbed us, but well recall the regular meetings with 'Pip' Davies for his shrewd and often merry observations on our work. One or two particular assignments were never to be forgotten - for me a close appraisal of Tennyson's 'In Memoriam' in full, the whole four years of it. Then, when I became a Senior I must present a 'thesis' of my own choice, which became 'The Value of the Aesthetic Desire', with Pip putting me to Edmund Burke on the Sublime and Beautiful and setting me to struggle with Schopenhauer and the world as Will and Idea - all of which made plain to me that much more was yet to be learned. Our forays to the Principal's own study snug in his 'quarters' revealed him masterly in a quiet way on the prose of R. L. Stevenson, the lesser known 'Virginibus Puerisque' and Aes Triplex', and truly enthusiastic in disentangling much of Robert Browning for us. Advanced Geography took me and three others to the very different study of W. T. Stephenson, known affectionately as 'Stevie, the Round the World Man'. Small but bursting with enthusiasm for his subject he was also electrifying with the Mathematics he took with other admiring groups. Exhilarating, demanding work with these very different scholarly men made Culham entirely worthwhile to me.

Our first full lecture was with the Vice-Principal, the Reverend Evelyn F. Brailey, a direct and impressive man, who stated that Methodology, Child Psychology, Class Management, Lesson Preparation and Presentation were his field and essential for everyone of us - so how best to ensure that what we teach stays? He proceeded then to an exposition of the Herbartian Method, that of Johann Friedrich Herbart, the German philosopher, whose scheme of lesson presentation we then noted rather than followed while attempting an assessment of the speaker, because we saw in him the completion of the ordained triumvirate–of Principal, Vice-Principal and 'Pip' Davies. We saw in them the ultimate management, which was supported by their carefully chosen monitorial system designed, as Napper Scull said, to ease the 'day-to-day running of things'.

By long custom the monitors were drawn from the Senior Year, headed by a *General Monitor*, mainly chosen now from the older men with Forces' experience. As an ex-regimental sergeant major our 'GM' had a quelling look for green-horns while entirely ignoring our existence otherwise; though I do recall him once in our lecture room for a session with our whole group to remind us that all regulations continued in force and that slackness, or attempts to evade them could lead to what, perhaps, we had already observed, namely, that 'x' from our ranks was suddenly not with us. 'One stroke of the pen' in the Principal's study had sufficed and would be wielded again should need arise. The cold eye and ram-rod stance implied that it was well that military experience had been called in here.

His minions, as Granville called them, were a series of monitors. First a *Senior Monitor* to supervise the Senior Lecture Room. Of him I saw nothing in my first year, but heard that during one evening of private study, when he should rather have been dining at high table, the Principal strode through the room as toast-making round the stove and a jolly sing-song were being 'enjoyed by all', on which the helpless *Senior Monitor* almost lost his post; then our *Junior Monitor* D. J. Webber, ever reasonable on his dais and popular as the football eleven's agile goal-keeper and 'Webby' to all; then a *Common Room Monitor* whose hours, poor man, were long and never the same and demanding too when preparing for a full college debate between protagonists never to be reconciled, or, much more flustering, the concert in which daring student Fox was programmed to sing, right before the Principal in the front seat. '*Give the devil his due, his friends are many, his foes are few*' and '*Take a pair of Sparkling Eyes*', this to be balanced by the VP's '*Mair, my Girl*'; then a very necessary *Chapel Monitor*, whose continuous concern was tracking down the occasional absentee, extracting the one shilling fine and safe-guarding the monies as slowly they increased and finally, two *Library Monitors*, whose first duty was to ascertain each new man's requirements of new text and other books as laid down, not forgetting the Canon's *Life of our Blessed Lord*, required for our course for gaining the Archbishop's Divinity Certificate. There came an early session when we went in file with the exact cash required to bear away our pile. Harry Botcherby, the Chief Monitor, was an efficient and kindly son of a Yorkshire headmaster who, through my Junior Year, saw to it that I should wear his shoes, as he said, 'when the time comes'.

I realised quite soon that we were as variegated a concourse in age, experience, personality and, probably, outlook as ever could have been called together to teach children, as the Principal himself had guardedly acknowledged in the first chapel meeting. Most of our Seniors had served in the Forces. Several had families living away. Service lore was the only lore of several. Of one it was said that David Lloyd George had helped him to win the war. The several one-year men mixed hardly at all, having the library as base, while some of the younger men were ex-public school boys of uneven conviction and quality who formed self-sufficient cliques. Added to these were even younger entrants such as Granville, the pining Herman Munday and myself and, shortly, the Welsh contingent of ex-shipwrights. We were quite the mixed company Napper Scull had said we would be. The Canon might well have had apprehensions in his rectory back in the Downs. The staff to guide us were mixed too - the three highly qualified ordained men and laymen of variable value. The Canon himself - Divinity, Browning, Tennyson, Shakespeare, the weekly essay - was masterly; the Vice-Principal, whose introductory lecture we had already attended, was a scholarly man of wide vision who in later years went to a bishopric; the Reverend R. Trevor Davies - Divinity, English Literature, History - a huge, quite young and jolly man, always affectionately known as 'Pip' who also took on advanced subjects, his immense learning and enthusiasm an inspiration in his seminars. He, the Canon and the Vice-Principal prepared us First Year students for sitting the Archbishop's Examination in Divinity to be passed within the year. 'Pip' must have jollied us along to good effect for me to achieve, along with most others, first class, for I recall a fearful struggle with the Epistle to the Galatians.

At my coming the staff lacked a full complement of laymen. R. R. Kimbell - physical Education, Music, including inspiring choral work - was established and invaluable. Some years ahead he became a principal himself. We had to wait a week or two for W. T. Stephenson, whose Geography and Mathematics were temporarily in the hands of the head of the nearby practising school who yielded them up with obvious relief - I recall that New Zealand was his long-suffering 'topic', as he called it, along with a liking for Maori place names. 'Stevie' was a great acquisition. His Maths, men homed in on him immediately and we Geography men waited on his every word, map and diagram. Besides, he proved to be the brilliant winger the college football eleven had signed for.

Art struggled throughout my stay at Culham in the care of an earnest Abingdon headmaster visiting on Saturday mornings. It has ever since amused me that the instant he discovered that I could draw 'fine hair-lines and curves' to equal his he recommended me to make Art my third advanced subject, leaving me to devise my own exercises in line and watercolour week by week. Only once did he contrive a 'subject' for me - a pair of much-used tennis shoes lying idly together. My result he said, 'quite thrilled him for their reality'. From all this astonishingly I acquired a Credit in the Board of Education's Final Examination in 1923.

Along with 'Stevie' arrived Joseph Smedley from Leeds University to take on the waiting Science men and also School Hygiene, compulsory for all. Since our seniors had had none so far of the latter he was confronted by full houses and soon it was plain that few apart from himself took him and the sessions in his lecture-theatre seriously. Harry Botcherby of the library owned a copy of the text used by the unsuspecting 'Joe' in his lecture preparations. Graciously Harry lent me this for private note-making, so that, with a ready co-operator I could concentrate on other work as Joe's lecture wound its way towards the bell: we called this 'Private study with Joe'. Perhaps with the group of men committed to his Science things were more fruitful and happy. For me they lived in a foreign land but for the amazing moment in 1922 when we packed his Science theatre to listen to the first ever radio broadcast from London. It is sad fact that the Principal had to wait until after I had completed my full two-year course and was gone to complete his staff with men of high calibre in Art and Science.

Whatever the circumstances the College must send out men who could teach, so the Vice-Principal's Methodology and all entailed in it took priority in our Lecture Room. At that time a class-teacher taught every subject in his class timetable, usually with no free preparation or marking time and expecting none. I had been doing it with varying success for more than a year. Yet I was surprised and unprepared for what was solemnly laid before us, that leading pupils from the 'known to the unknown' must be done in firmly prescribed stages and by the tenets of Johann Friedrich Herbart, the German philosopher. Every lesson had to be an entity - aim clearly stated in your preparation book with the steps, or stages laid out as it developed to a final statement, or application stage, as to what practically the pupils would be required to do to prove that knowledge had been absorbed. This had to be displayed in your school-practice book for every lesson with the book open to the Master of Method and to the heads of schools who made teaching-practice available.

It was said that one local village headmaster, zealous for Herbart, ensured that students practising under his auspices, should adhere exactly to the lesson stages by sounding a bell himself at their precise moments, with a special sound for the all-important final application stage. It may well have been this committee man who, on receiving first-time students on a Monday morning, declined their proffered hands saying: 'Don't want your hands - I want your books'.

So teaching-practice was always approached with interest. For a spell you were un-cloistered and the unknown lay before you often with surprises. Wonder of wonders, in your second week the head might say that he would like to claim your services at your course's end, or, better still, two weeks of bliss practising with the pupils of a delightfully understanding lady teacher. This happened to one of our ever hopeful senior men, so that marriage followed the moment he was free.

Men who had done no teaching before Culham spent twelve weeks in the practising-schools, those who had already taught spent six weeks, all in fortnightly spells, in Abingdon Council and Abingdon Church of England schools, several large village schools in the vicinity, or in the small practising-school adjoining the college. The latter drew to it able boys aiming for grammar school, or 'common entrance'. My first teaching practice was in Abingdon Council School where my elderly, long-experienced class teacher saw that 'discipline was kept' while her young practitioner endeavoured to adhere to Herbartian principles with uneven success, especially on market days, for the school stood close to the town cattle-pens. Next to shouting drovers, pigs were the most demanding of attention. No tutor came near me, the headmaster initialled my book, the good lady appeared relatively happy with my short tenure. I felt I had gained little, except that her neat method of enrolling her pupils for the distribution and collection of books and material was worth remembering.

Later, two more of my weeks were spent comfortably in the college practising-school, a quite peaceful episode. 'Bread' Evetts, the headmaster, he who had caused many a yawn when 'taking' Geography with us, was a mild and soothing man who had made his small school almost unnoticed standing college-style only a few yards from our walls. My class had been smoothed or soothed into a smiling readiness for everything I could do for them by way of Herbart, while for most of my lessons Headmaster Evetts sat at the side breathing assurance, saying at the end of my stay: 'I have put you on my list', meaning what I could not fathom, for I knew that lessons when I drew strongly on A. C. Walter and J. T. Read had been my best. Perhaps I learned something invaluable – the importance of a persistently quiet demeanour before a class – I can think of nothing more. My last practice at the end of my final year was the most useful. It was in Abingdon C of E School with a class of eleven and twelve year old boys whose gentle lady teacher could only just 'hold' them, so that the headmaster frequently looked in to scowl until there was silence. To me he said: 'Do what you think best with them'. On this I abandoned my lesson notes, especially the 'question and answer' techniques of such as our Master of Method and his German guru, putting them down at once to protracted written work, e.g. the sentence *They're helping their mother over there*, to be done fifty times in best handwriting; similarly with all multiplication tables done backwards and then mixed as indicated on the blackboard. All I asked of their teacher was the provision of all plain scrap-paper available while she gratefully 'caught up' with her marking. Variations on this saw them pretty weary by the end of each day, so in the last period I read to them from '*Captains Courageous*', encouraging them to sing with me, *Don't cry little fish – little fish, don't cry.* The head looked in on us when this began, reached for my lesson-book, hummed with us for a bit and then wrote in it one word – 'Noted' saying, 'Keep them busy.' I quietly said the same many times to the relieved lady, recalling now my first London headmaster's words to a similar class he gave me as a young teacher puzzled by city boys: 'Bodies busy, not busy-bodies, eh?'

As expected a Government Inspector looked in on me in the second week to approve, or question, my teaching-mark. He arrived during an art lesson. We were drawing curiously arranged garden flowerpots. Had he wished to see my non-Herbartian lesson notes on this he would have read: 'Aim – to depict in colour three earthernware flowerpots, variously arranged to provide thirty-six different viewpoints, including my own from the blackboard'. He wrote 'Examined' against this, looked at what we had all done so far, saying quietly to me, 'Keep going' and left, presumably to confer with the head, not forgetting to give our busily marking and correcting lady an encouraging smile.

Statement of aim for art-work was often difficult if not impossible. In desperation one student wrote, or it was said that he wrote: 'Aim – to exercise the smaller muscles of the hand.' No aspect of Culham life was more fruitful than teaching-practice in providing memorable moments and not least was my pleasure in having had a really understanding headmaster unobtrusively at hand for a practice that had a big question-mark over it from day one.

I had been reminded that the Vice-Principal's lectures on lesson presentation, class control, the problem pupil and teaching techniques, were highly academic, though his Child Psychology Course yielded useful insights and, indeed, on one occasion provided a helpful and amusing one on himself. In a discussion on concentration, having in mind my ever-memorable Emma Rickards of Standard Three in Steeple Claydon School. I mentioned the difficulty of a male teacher of a mixed form of adolescents when a girl develops a fixation on him, then known as a 'pash'. I see now his sudden smile as he said: 'Believe it or not it happened several times to me. I never failed to effect a cure for the sufferer by sitting her for her work full-time right in front of my desk. When, as always happened, there came after a while a request for a change of position, I knew that the crisis was passed'. Whereupon, of course, anticipating A. S. Neill, he then turned to the problem teacher.

I knew that he must lead us to teach intelligently and thoroughly what J. T. Read called the 'hum-drum' stuff. I kept to myself the more inspirational things he and A. C. Walter regularly did, in which Herbart, as then applied, had no part. Particularly I remembered one of J. T. Read's Friday afternoon picture-recognition sessions, when, at the end, he said to Lona and me, his young teachers-to-be: 'The most worthwhile things are better caught than taught. None of this is measurable.'

The many lectures we attended in two years were bound to have their occasional unexpected and interesting moments. Those of the Canon, the VP and Pip Davies preparing us for the Archbishop's Divinity Examination, however, were sober affairs in which memory was going to be all. However our year included one or two strong-minded men of non-conformist persuasion, so sometimes there could be a challenge, a red-faced student on his feet, Bible in hand, the lecturer tight-lipped and patient, saying eventually: 'After the lecture, dear man, see me personally.'

But nothing of this equalled the small sensation I myself caused in a Divinity lecture of the Canon's when searching for elusive words in response to a direct question to me, I spoke of the three 'aspects' of the Trinity, for the Canon, for a second, to appear almost stunned. Coldly he then said: 'Aspects, aspects, *aspects*, Chapman?' I see again his trembling stance as he continued: 'You in your special study are inevitably a man of words. Pray attend with the utmost care to every single word you use.' The difficult moment passed after I had been solemnly put right, but he eyed me warily to the lecture's end. What was Bishop Samuel Wilberforce's Culham College, Oxon., of 1922 nourishing?

I recall with amused pleasure the close of the course. A private paddock next to the chapel was opened to us for a week of final revision and there we repaired to test each other and refresh our memory of our notes. It was June - we reclined in the shade or strolled to and fro, privileged revisers, preparing for a time honoured act peculiar to Culham. On the morning of the examination we formed a file facing the twelve cypresses alongside the chapel wall for the purpose of 'Kicking Judas'. Eleven trees stood straight and tall, but Judas, the end one, was markedly stunted if not a weakling. His bole had been ceremoniously kicked before examinations by countless students and now, solemnly one by one, we kicked him too, I quietly murmuring: 'Nothing on Galatians, please'.

This ended my year as a Junior, when our Seniors, their Finals imminent, also kicked Judas, sat their examination and then, quite

The Library of Culham College in the early 1920s.
Photograph: Culham Educational Foundation

swiftly, were gone. My Senior Year began in the following September, placing Frank Dann and me in the library as Monitors there and Granville, Herman Munday and others in positions of importance. Later we 'library men' were made jointly responsible for producing the college magazine. For this, to accompany the editorial, the Principal gave me an original poem in his own handwriting proclaiming his quiet scholarship and assurance. This poem rests now, among other Culham memorabilia with the Culham Educational Foundation in Abingdon. Other advantages of monitorial status were for me a move to a cubicle in Major dormitory with a view down the main drive, such as Napper's, and admission to the exclusiveness of the Monitors' Common Room, characterised for me by much talk and flying ping-pong balls.

The Canon was not only an occasional poet but a scholar and 'Richard the Third' in our year's syllabus had just begun under his aegis, and was to be a thorough business. This led to a famous occasion in the lecture room. First everyone was made aware of the ancient stage setting, next there must be a reading right through preparatory to a close study of the text. One morning therefore he entered book in hand while we were ready with copies open at Act One, Scene Two, the point last reached. He mounted the rostrum, head held high and read slowly and resonantly: 'Enter the corpse of King Henry the Sixth, borne in an open coffin: Gentlemen bearing halberds to guard it and Lady Anne as mourner'. He paused now looking us over and said: 'Stand up Cole, if you please. As we have heard nothing of note from you lately you shall be Lady Anne for us today. You are a dreadfully distraught lady, so let us hear it in your voice'. Diffidently Cole rose, clutching his book, but straightened up for the Canon's eye and visage were not to be denied and so began in the lilting tones he had brought from West Wales: 'Set down, set down your honourable load if honour may be shrouded in a hearse,' and on and on, the Canon nodding encouragement, until he reached the lines demanding full histrionic power as poor distracted Anne when his h's deserted him and he shrieked: 'O, cursed be the 'and which made these 'ateful 'oles - cursed by the 'eart that 'ad the 'eart to do it!' On this the Canon said coldly and evenly: 'Stop - we all knew Lancaster to be newly and bloodily slain, but were given no warning that Shakespeare himself was to be laid low this very morning. Sit down, sir, for goodness sake.'

The Student's Garden of Culham College in the early 1920s.
Photograph: Culham Educational Foundation

The Principal and the Diocesan authorities with the generous help of past students had acquired adjacent land for a large sports field, enabling the Welsh contingent to put Culham men on the local rugby-football map. The college proceeded next on something more directly educational. They persuaded the farmer whose land adjoined a long straight stretch of college boundary wall to sell a strip wide enough to make a series of small gardens which Rural Sciencemen would cultivate in order to take expertise into the schools. 'Joe' Smedley readily took this in hand, so pioneer work began with the making of a path marking the limit of the college's acquisition. It had to be well-bedded and being about three hundred yards long required all the student help Joe could muster. He led with great enthusiasm, not hesitating to point out the high professionalism of his work. Students likely to be granted gardens were his busiest diggers. However, when the path was nearing completion the farmer, his overseer and a land surveyor with chain and paper plan arrived to stop the work. Unhappily Joe had incorrectly aligned his path - there was incontrovertible proof that the college was taking a long slice of land to which it had no title. The farmer therefore demanded that what was his must be restored in time for the next ploughing and the path made as on the plan which Joe in his haste had failed to check. So he and a diminished band of students began at once the back-aching work which postponed the provision of anything like promising gardens until I was about to leave. Still Joe was not deterred. He went about the college to recruit men to replace those who had defaulted but with small success. Men said directly: 'Will you be in full charge, sir?' and then shook their heads. One said: 'Well, sir, God Almighty first planted a garden and so far as I am concerned He can get on with this one.' Very slowly the work went on. One morning 'Pip' Davies paid the workers a visit, saying to the perspiring Joe: 'Just to ask you to put my name down for the grape harvest, you busy man.' I was not surprised that soon after my course ended Joe left to become head of a country school somewhere - perhaps with gardens ready-made?

In lecture-room and pulpit ever commanding and erudite, the Principal was for long periods unseen. Only occasionally was his dark figure to be observed about the college. The tap of his walking stick in the cloisters would awake swift interest and sometimes surprise as two shapes in identical black appeared, he leading and his wife some six paces behind. The same formation sufficed for a country walk and for one such walk on a summer Sunday afternoon along the towpath of the Thames, its twinkling water and changing interests invitingly near. It happened that in blessed extension time two of our students were on the river at this time gently sculling along a happy boat-load of local young ladies. In the same line of travel, with their backs to the walkers, the rowers unwittingly drew level with the Principal and his wife and smoothly passed alongside, when within two further strokes of their oars rhythm was utterly and almost disastrously lost, the ladies crying out in understandable alarm, while the walkers paced steadily on appearing to have noticed nothing of the incident. Yet in 'Notices' after evening chapel it was given out that the Principal wished to meet in his study at nine a.m. the next day 'the two adventurers seen to be carrying contraband goods along the river this afternoon' - the price was four weeks' 'gating' in glorious May–June weather. The grimness of the Principal's face over this period was proof enough that the regulations regarding female persons would be rigidly adhered to. So it was unfortunate that at this time our colleague, Herman Munday, took courage, so it was said, to seek permission to invite his fiancée in for a brief viewing of the places in which he toiled and pined. Three times he ventured and three times he quailed at the Principal's bell-push, retreating once again to his lonely writing desk in the Lecture Room.

We were in the final weeks of our courses now when it was deemed necessary that we should have some experience of light craft for schools. Expert male instructors were brought in for half-day sessions, once a week, of book-binding or clay-modelling, which of course quickly became 'clay-binding' - you opted for one or the other. I chose the clay, remembering my speciality in plasticine - elephants, camels, igloos, kralls, log cabins, for Lily Chapman in Easy Claydon School long ago. At Culham I played safe by producing 'creatures which never were'.

At this time too, our R. R. Kimbell, the enterprising and popular music and physical education man, made acquaintance with country dance people in Oxford who would teach us dances we could take into the schools when, soon, we would leave for the outside world. No one knows how it came about that the Principal agreed for once that for expert tuition it was essential for a lady to take us in hand. Prohibition was waived for the duration of the course and there arrived from Oxford the most delightfully feminine person ever to be seen. She was ballerina-like, light as a feather, but crisp in command and gently patient, with the sweetest encouraging smiles, to those who were interested to learn. Suddenly that was the whole year, drawn as intoxicated moths to a candle. As patient seated wall-flowers we lined the walls of the Common Room as she selected a ready manly partner to demonstrate basic steps, taking care to smile upon someone completely other for the next and then another. It became interesting now to observe 'Ikey' Isaacs, our ever-ready Lothario, beaming upon her while being entirely overlooked, but ready, should a tiny handkerchief fall, or a helping hand be sought. But nothing fluttered from the small lithe form, just merry chuckles as she daintily evaded continuous danger. When it came to choosing an 'eight' to learn a first dance twenty men arose at once to her delightful laughter, but eight it must be and she chose them herself, making fretful Ikey number eight, though by her quick glance it seemed she would have preferred to enlist my tall colleague and long-time friend William Penrose - 'Bill' - Nash, who shrugged and smiled. We then learned the simple Sellenger's Round, Kimbell himself at the piano, tinkling the catchy old tune, setting feet going throughout the hall. But now another yearning eight must be added and Ikey the leader whereon his side-winks to cronies not yet on the floor were outrageous in the extreme. But the session had to end and there at once was Kimbell with her light wrap put to her light shoulders and bearing her away to the Canon's quarters while men stood bewildered that in that sacrosanct pile somewhere there was a changing-room provided. Men walked away as if awakened from a dream and as in a dream a whole week of lectures, seminars, private study and 'usual arrangements' slowly passed before the dear lady came again. Now it was to perfect six sets of Sellenger's Round and to begin 'Gathering Peascods' and 'All on a Summer's Day' with Bill swiftly chosen to lead each dance. These happily done she tripped lightly right away, for the Principal's waiver was strictly temporary, leaving a sort of wistfulness amongst us, which was only relieved by an invitation from Oxford for keen new dancers to join a full day's folk-dance festival on the lawns of New College. That happy Saturday stays in my mind along with the magical moments when suddenly, as indeed it was, a sylph-like form and merry laugh lifted Culham for once completely out of its staid old self, our final reward the words of our lady as she tripped amongst the dancers saying that her 'boys from Culham' were quite the most lightsome of the men.

After such excitements in that late summer term Culham for me seems to have ambled towards July and Finals when I was again with

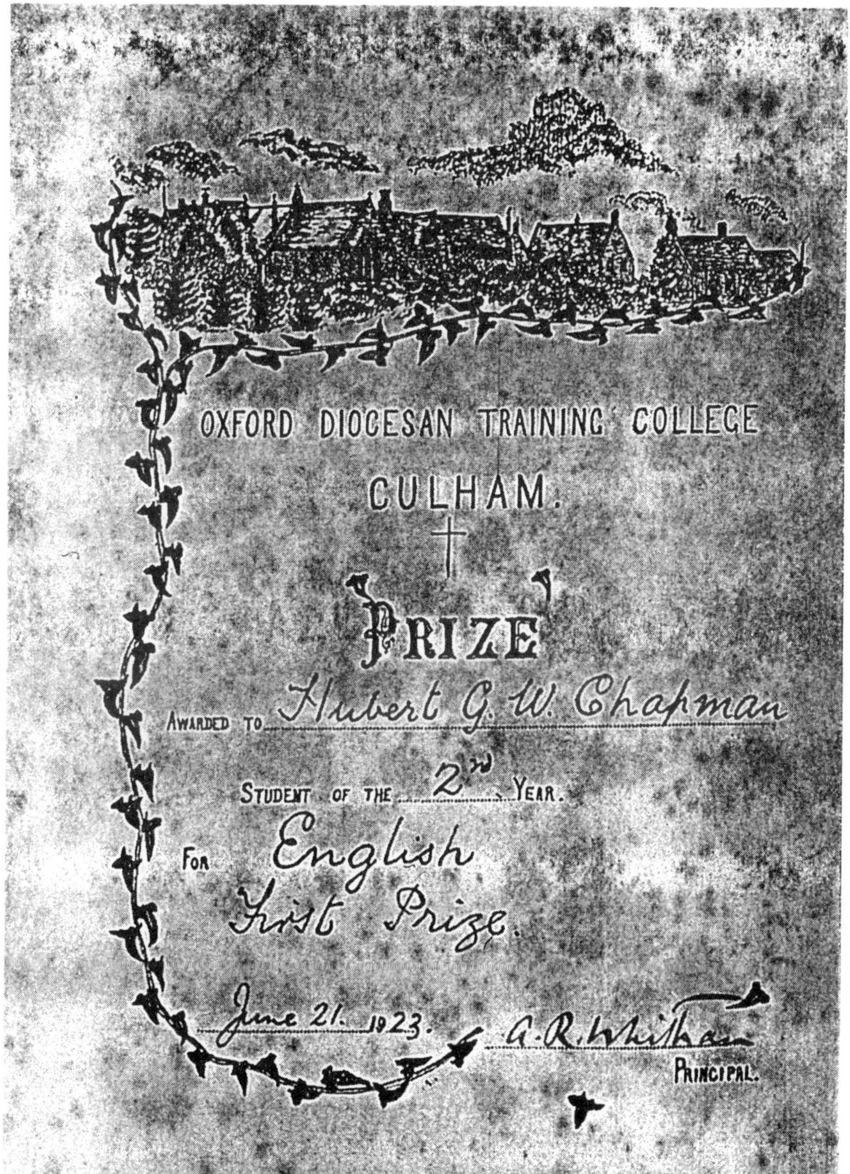

Bookplate from a set of Shakespeare's Plays awarded to Hubert Chapman in 1923 as First Prize for English in his second year at Culham.

my peers in the little paddock for a week of revision and revision and revision, with for me urgent refreshment of my knowledge of the set work on the major poets. We strolled to and fro and, for a change, sat in the green shade of its trees with the twelve apostles darkly watching and Judas resignedly waiting. Then on the morning of the first paper I joined in the meanest onslaught he had ever suffered, all pointing out that, anyway, the recent Great War had afforded him fine respite. When the examinations were over London school inspectors arrived at the college to interview the large body of men who had applied to be placed in the list of First Appointments established by that go-ahead Local Education Authority under the directorship then of renowned Sir Robert Blair. It transpired, though it was unknown to Granville and me for a long time, that Walter Wallace Bartlett, who had attended Culham at the time of the Canon's coming as the new reforming Principal and was now a headmaster in South London, had applied directly to the Canon for two likely young fellows to help him initiate a modified Dalton Private Study Plan in the school to which recently he had been elevated for the purpose. Granville Jackson and I were nominated and so, Culham, at last behind us, in late August we arrived in Bartlett's school in Herne Hill, South London, with whatever Culham had bestowed on us to help him.

London Schoolboys. The author's first class as a fully fledged qualified teacher at Jessop Road Boys' School (Headmaster W. W. Bartlett), Herne Hill, South London in 1923. Photograph: Hubert Chapman

It is a strange fact that my last days and departure from my old college remain almost blank in my memory while my first and many others are quite clear.

But one vivid final moment stands clear, how on walking to Culham Station for the last time, Granville and I stopped long to contemplate Bishop Wilberforce's pile, 'purpose fixed in ever-memorable stone', others hurrying on – Bill Nash for a strange school in West Yorkshire; Herman Munday for nearby Water Perry and his patient love; my co-mate Frank Dann of the library in haste for the Central Canada he had long dreamed about and where soon he would find a teaching place to last him a school lifetime.

Should you pass that way tomorrow there solidly the college still stands, but now as the Schola Europaea, which it became when 1979 brought for ever the closure of Culham as a training college for teachers. It is a special delight to me that it continues as one of a group of innovatory residential schools established over Europe for the education together of young people, bright girls and boys of different nationalities and diverse languages, some of whom may already have become leaders in many different ways in their own countries – perhaps even in changing Europe itself.

What the saintly shades of Bishop Wilberforce and the Canon may be saying about such a remarkable change of use as this can only be pondered and surmised.

Culham College from the air in the 1930s.
Photograph: Culham Educational Foundation

Books Published by THE BOOK CASTLE

JOURNEYS INTO BEDFORDSHIRE: Anthony Mackay.
Foreword by The Marquess of Tavistock, Woburn Abbey.
A lavish book of over 150 evocative ink drawings.

CHILTERN ARCHAEOLOGY: RECENT WORK:
A Handbook for the Next Decade: edited by Robin Holgate.
The latest views, results and excavations by twenty-three leading archaeologists throughout the Chilterns.

COUNTRYSIDE CYCLING IN BEDFORDSHIRE, BUCKINGHAMSHIRE and HERTFORDSHIRE: Mick Payne.
Twenty rides on- and off-road for all the family.

LOCAL WALKS: South Bedfordshire and North Chilterns:
Vaughan Basham. Twenty-seven thematic circular walks.

LOCAL WALKS: North and Mid-Bedfordshire:
Vaughan Basham. Twenty-five thematic circular walks.

CHILTERN WALKS: Hertfordshire, Bedfordshire and North Buckinghamshire: Nick Moon.
CHILTERN WALKS: Buckinghamshire: Nick Moon.
CHILTERN WALKS: Oxfordshire and West Buckinghamshire: Nick Moon.
A trilogy of circular walks, in association with the Chiltern Society. Each volume contains thirty circular walks.

OXFORDSHIRE WALKS:
Oxford, the Cotswolds and the Cherwell Valley: Nick Moon.
OXFORDSHIRE WALKS:
Oxford, the Downs and the Thames Valley: Nick Moon.
Two volumes that complement Chiltern Walks: Oxfordshire and complete coverage of the county, in association with the Oxford Fieldpaths Society. Thirty circular walks in each.

FOLK: Characters and Events in the History of Bedfordshire and Northamptonshire: Vivienne Evans.
Anthology about people of yesteryear – arranged alphabetically by village or town.

JOHN BUNYAN: HIS LIFE AND TIMES: Vivienne Evans.
Foreword by the Bishop of Bedford. Preface by Terry Waite.
Bedfordshire's most famous son set in his seventeenth century context.

LEGACIES:
Tales and Legends of Bedfordshire and Hertfordshire:
Vic Lea. Twenty-five mysteries and stories based on fact, including Luton Town Football Club. Many photographs.

ECHOES: Tales and Legends of Bedfordshire and Hertfordshire: Vic Lea.
Thirty, compulsively retold historical incidents.

MYTHS and WITCHES, PEOPLE and POLITICS: Tales from Four Shires: Bucks., Beds., Herts., and Northants.: John Houghton.
Anthology of strange but true historical events.

ECCENTRICS and VILLAINS, HAUNTINGS and HEROES: Tales from Four Shires: Northants., Beds., Bucks. and Herts.: John Houghton.
True incidents and curious events covering one thousand years.

THE RAILWAY AGE IN BEDFORDSHIRE: Fred Cockman.
Classic, illustrated acount of early railway history.

SWANS IN MY KITCHEN: The Story of a Swan Sanctuary: Lis Dorer. Foreword by Dr Philip Burton. Updated edition.
Tales of her dedication to the survival of these beautiful birds through her sanctuary near Hemel Hempstead.

WHIPSNADE WILD ANIMAL PARK: 'MY AFRICA': Lucy Pendar.
Foreword by Andrew Forbes. Introduction by Gerald Durrell.
Inside story of sixty years of the Park's animals and people – full of anecdotes, photographs and drawings.

DUNSTABLE WITH THE PRIORY, 1100–1550: Vivienne Evans.
Dramatic growth of Henry I's important new town around a major crossroads.

DUNSTABLE DECADE: THE EIGHTIES: A Collection of Photographs: Pat Lovering.
A souvenir book of nearly 300 pictures of people and events in the 1980s.

DUNSTABLE IN DETAIL: Nigel Benson.
A hundred of the town's buildings and features, plus town trail map.

OLD DUNSTABLE: Bill Twaddle.
A new edition of this collection of early photographs.

BOURNE and BRED: A Dunstable Boyhood Between the Wars: Colin Bourne.
An elegantly written, well-illustrated book capturing the spirit of the town over fifty years ago.

ROYAL HOUGHTON: Pat Lovering.
Illustrated history of Houghton Regis from the earliest times to the present.

BEDFORDSHIRE'S YESTERYEARS Vol. 1:
The Family, Childhood and Schooldays:
Brenda Fraser-Newstead.
Unusual early 20th century reminiscences, with private photographs.

BEDFORDSHIRE'S YESTERYEARS Vol. 2:
The Rural Scene: Brenda Fraser-Newstead.
Vivid first-hand accounts of country life two or three generations ago.

BEDFORDSHIRE'S YESTERYEARS Vol. 3:
Craftsmen and Trades People: Brenda Fraser-Newstead.
Fascinating recollections over several generations practising many vanishing crafts and trades.

PUBS and PINTS:
The Story of Luton's Public Houses and Breweries:
Stuart Smith.
Three hundred rare photographs illustrate this detailed account of the town's important brewing industry and retail beer outlets, past and present.

THE CHANGING FACE OF LUTON:
An Illustrated History:
Stephen Bunker, Robin Holgate and Marian Nichols.
Luton's development from earliest times to the present busy industrial town. Illustrated in colour and monochrome. The three authors from Luton Museum are all experts in local history, archaeology, crafts and social history.

THE MEN WHO WORE STRAW HELMETS:
Policing Luton, 1840–1974: Tom Madigan.
Meticulously chronicled history; dozens of rare photographs; author served in Luton Police for nearly fifty years.

BETWEEN THE HILLS:
The Story of Lilley, a Chiltern Village: Roy Pinnock.
A priceless piece of our heritage – the rural beauty remains but the customs and way of life described here have largely disappeared.

GLEANINGS REVISITED:
Nostalgic Thoughts of a Bedfordshire's Farmer's Boy:
E W O'Dell.
His own sketches and early photographs adorn this lively account of rural Bedfordshire in days gone by.

FARM OF MY CHILDHOOD, 1925–1947: Mary Roberts.
An almost vanished lifestyle on a remote farm near Flitwick.

THE TALL HITCHIN SERGEANT:
A Victorian Crime Novel based on fact: Edgar Newman.
Mixes real police officers and authentic background with an exciting storyline.

THE TALL HITCHIN INSPECTOR'S CASEBOOK:
A Victorian Crime Novel based on fact: Edgar Newman.
Worthies of the time encounter more archetypal villains.

LEAFING THROUGH LITERATURE: Writer's Lives in Hertfordshire and Bedfordshire: David Carroll.
Illustrated short biographies of many famous authors and their connections with these counties.

THROUGH VISITORS' EYES:
A Bedfordshire Anthology: edited by Simon Houfe.
Impressions of the county by famous visitors over the last four centuries, thematically arranged and illustrated with line drawings.

THE HILL OF THE MARTYR: An Architectural History of St. Albans Abbey: Eileen Roberts.
Scholarly and readable chronological narrative history of Hertfordshire and Bedfordshire's famous cathedral. Fully illustrated with photographs and plans.

SPECIALLY FOR CHILDREN

VILLA BELOW THE KNOLLS:
A Story of Roman Britain: Michael Dundrow.
An exciting adventure for young John in Totternhoe and Dunstable two thousand years ago.

ADVENTURE ON THE KNOLLS:
A Story of Iron Age Britain: Michael Dundrow.
Excitement on Totternhoe Knolls as ten-year-old John finds himself back in those dangerous times, confronting Julius Caesar and his army.

THE RAVENS:
One Boy Against the Might of Rome: James Dyer.
On the Barton Hills and in the south-east of England as the men of the great fort of Ravensburgh (near Hexton) confront the invaders.

Further titles are in preparation.
All the above are available via any bookshop, or from the publisher and bookseller

THE BOOK CASTLE
12 Church Street, Dunstable Bedfordshire, LU5 4RU
Tel: (01582) 605670

Broken Window

The House of Jack the Ripper book 1

AMY CROSS

First published by Dark Season Books,
United Kingdom, 2017

Copyright © 2017 Amy Cross

All rights reserved. This book is a work of fiction.
Names, characters, places, incidents and businesses are
the product of the author's imagination or are
used fictitiously. Any resemblance to actual persons,
living or dead, or to actual events or locates,
is entirely coincidental.

ISBN: 9781549533167

Also available in e-book format.

www.amycross.com